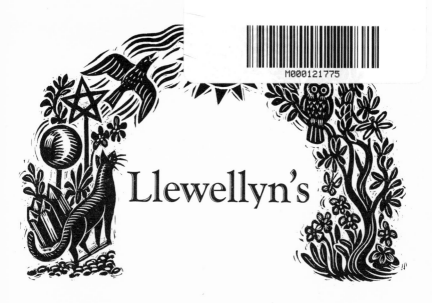

Llewellyn's

Witches' Datebook

2007

Featuring

Art by Jennifer Hewitson
Text by Elizabeth Barrette, Dallas Jennifer Cobb,
Ellen Dugan, Emely Flak, Magenta Griffith,
James Kambos, Lynn Smythe, K. D. Spitzer,
and Abby Willowroot

ISBN 0-7387-0330-3

2007

JANUARY
S	M	T	W	T	F	S
	1	2	3	4	5	6
7	8	9	10	11	12	13
14	15	16	17	18	19	20
21	22	23	24	25	26	27
28	29	30	31			

FEBRUARY
S	M	T	W	T	F	S
				1	2	3
4	5	6	7	8	9	10
11	12	13	14	15	16	17
18	19	20	21	22	23	24
25	26	27	28			

MARCH
S	M	T	W	T	F	S
				1	2	3
4	5	6	7	8	9	10
11	12	13	14	15	16	17
18	19	20	21	22	23	24
25	26	27	28	29	30	31

APRIL
S	M	T	W	T	F	S
1	2	3	4	5	6	7
8	9	10	11	12	13	14
15	16	17	18	19	20	21
22	23	24	25	26	27	28
29	30					

MAY
S	M	T	W	T	F	S
		1	2	3	4	5
6	7	8	9	10	11	12
13	14	15	16	17	18	19
20	21	22	23	24	25	26
27	28	29	30	31		

JUNE
S	M	T	W	T	F	S
					1	2
3	4	5	6	7	8	9
10	11	12	13	14	15	16
17	18	19	20	21	22	23
24	25	26	27	28	29	30

JULY
S	M	T	W	T	F	S
1	2	3	4	5	6	7
8	9	10	11	12	13	14
15	16	17	18	19	20	21
22	23	24	25	26	27	28
29	30	31				

AUGUST
S	M	T	W	T	F	S
			1	2	3	4
5	6	7	8	9	10	11
12	13	14	15	16	17	18
19	20	21	22	23	24	25
26	27	28	29	30	31	

SEPTEMBER
S	M	T	W	T	F	S
						1
2	3	4	5	6	7	8
9	10	11	12	13	14	15
16	17	18	19	20	21	22
23	24	25	26	27	28	29
30						

OCTOBER
S	M	T	W	T	F	S
	1	2	3	4	5	6
7	8	9	10	11	12	13
14	15	16	17	18	19	20
21	22	23	24	25	26	27
28	29	30	31			

NOVEMBER
S	M	T	W	T	F	S
				1	2	3
4	5	6	7	8	9	10
11	12	13	14	15	16	17
18	19	20	21	22	23	24
25	26	27	28	29	30	

DECEMBER
S	M	T	W	T	F	S
						1
2	3	4	5	6	7	8
9	10	11	12	13	14	15
16	17	18	19	20	21	22
23	24	25	26	27	28	29
30	31					

2008

JANUARY
S	M	T	W	T	F	S
		1	2	3	4	5
6	7	8	9	10	11	12
13	14	15	16	17	18	19
20	21	22	23	24	25	26
27	28	29	30	31		

FEBRUARY
S	M	T	W	T	F	S
					1	2
3	4	5	6	7	8	9
10	11	12	13	14	15	16
17	18	19	20	21	22	23
24	25	26	27	28	29	

MARCH
S	M	T	W	T	F	S
						1
2	3	4	5	6	7	8
9	10	11	12	13	14	15
16	17	18	19	20	21	22
23	24	25	26	27	28	29
30	31					

APRIL
S	M	T	W	T	F	S
		1	2	3	4	5
6	7	8	9	10	11	12
13	14	15	16	17	18	19
20	21	22	23	24	25	26
27	28	29	30			

MAY
S	M	T	W	T	F	S
				1	2	3
4	5	6	7	8	9	10
11	12	13	14	15	16	17
18	19	20	21	22	23	24
25	26	27	28	29	30	31

JUNE
S	M	T	W	T	F	S
1	2	3	4	5	6	7
8	9	10	11	12	13	14
15	16	17	18	19	20	21
22	23	24	25	26	27	28
29	30					

JULY
S	M	T	W	T	F	S
		1	2	3	4	5
6	7	8	9	10	11	12
13	14	15	16	17	18	19
20	21	22	23	24	25	26
27	28	29	30	31		

AUGUST
S	M	T	W	T	F	S
					1	2
3	4	5	6	7	8	9
10	11	12	13	14	15	16
17	18	19	20	21	22	23
24	25	26	27	28	29	30
31						

SEPTEMBER
S	M	T	W	T	F	S
	1	2	3	4	5	6
7	8	9	10	11	12	13
14	15	16	17	18	19	20
21	22	23	24	25	26	27
28	29	30				

OCTOBER
S	M	T	W	T	F	S
			1	2	3	4
5	6	7	8	9	10	11
12	13	14	15	16	17	18
19	20	21	22	23	24	25
26	27	28	29	30	31	

NOVEMBER
S	M	T	W	T	F	S
						1
2	3	4	5	6	7	8
9	10	11	12	13	14	15
16	17	18	19	20	21	22
23	24	25	26	27	28	29
30						

DECEMBER
S	M	T	W	T	F	S
	1	2	3	4	5	6
7	8	9	10	11	12	13
14	15	16	17	18	19	20
21	22	23	24	25	26	27
28	29	30	31			

Llewellyn's *Witches' Datebook 2007* © 2006 by Llewellyn Worldwide. 2143 Wooddale Dr., Dept. 0-7387-0330-3, Woodbury, MN 55125-2989. All rights reserved. No part of this publication may be reproduced in any form without the permission of the publisher except for quotations used in critical reviews. Llewellyn is a registered trademark of Llewellyn Worldwide, Ltd.

Editing/design by Ed Day

Cover illustration and interior art © 2006 by Jennifer Hewitson

Art on chapter openings © 2006 by Jennifer Hewitson

Cover design by Anne Marie Garrison

Art direction by Lynne Menturweck

Table of Contents

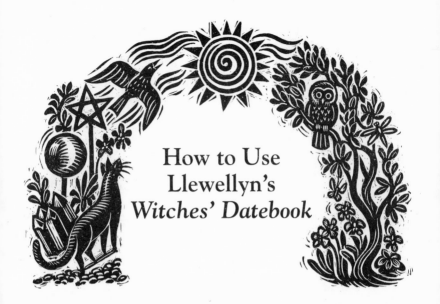

How to Use Llewellyn's Witches' Datebook

Welcome to Llewellyn's *Witches' Datebook 2007*! This datebook was designed especially for Witches, Pagans, and magical people. Use it to plan sabbat celebrations, magic, Full Moon rites, and even dentist and doctor appointments. Below is a symbol key to some of the features of this datebook.

Moon Quarters: The Moon's cycle is divided into four quarters, which are noted in the calendar pages along with their exact times. When the Moon changes quarter, both quarters are listed, as well as the time of the change. In addition, a symbol for the new quarter is placed where the numeral for the date usually appears.

Moon in the Signs: Approximately every two and a half days the Moon moves from one zodiac sign to the next. The sign that the Moon is in at the beginning of the day (midnight Eastern Standard Time) is noted next to the quarter listing. If the Moon changes signs that day, there will be a notation saying "☽ enters" followed by the symbol for the sign it is entering.

Moon Void-of-Course: Just before the Moon enters a new sign it will make one final aspect (angular relationship) to another planet. Between that last aspect and the entrance of the Moon into the next sign it is said to be void-of-course. Activities begun when the Moon is void-of-course rarely come to fruition, or they turn out very differently than planned.

PLANETARY MOVEMENT: When a planet or asteroid moves from one sign into another, this change (called an *ingress*) is noted on the calendar pages with the exact time. The Moon and Sun are considered planets in this case. The planets (except for the Sun and Moon) can also appear to move backward as seen from the Earth. This is called a *planetary retrograde*, and is noted on the calendar pages with the symbol ℞. When the planet begins to move forward, or direct, again, it is marked D, and the time is also noted.

PLANTING AND HARVESTING DAYS: The best days for planting and harvesting are noted on the calendar pages with a seedling icon (planting) and a basket icon (harvesting).

TIME ZONE CHANGES: The times and dates of all astrological phenomena in this datebook are based on Eastern time. If you live outside of the Eastern time zone, you will need to make the following changes: Pacific Time subtract three hours; Mountain Time subtract two hours; Central Time subtract one hour; and Alaska/Hawaii subtract five hours. All data is adjusted for Daylight Saving Time.

Planets

☉	Sun	
☽	Moon	
☿	Mercury	
♀	Venus	
♂	Mars	
♃	Jupiter	
♄	Saturn	
♅	Uranus	

♆	Neptune
♇	Pluto
⚷	Chiron
⚳	Ceres
⚴	Pallas
⚵	Juno
⚶	Vesta

Signs

♈	Aries	♐	Sagittarius
♉	Taurus	♑	Capricorn
♊	Gemini	♒	Aquarius
♋	Cancer	♓	Pisces
♌	Leo		
♍	Virgo		
♎	Libra		
♏	Scorpio		

Motion

℞	Retrograde
D	Direct

1st Quarter/New Moon ☽
2nd Quarter ☽

3rd Quarter/Full Moon ☺
4th Quarter ☽

☽ **Tuesday** ← Day and date
1st ♎ ← Moon's quarter and sign
2nd Quarter 4:01 am ← Moon quarter change
☽ v/c 4:01 am ← Moon void-of-course
☽ enters ♏ 9:30 am ← Moon sign change/ingress
♄ ℞ 10:14 am ← Planetary retrograde
Color: Gray ← Color of the day

Planting day → 🌱

Harvesting day → 🧺

Night of Hecate
by K. D. Spitzer

Hecate is known as the Goddess of Witches and of magic, the dark of the Moon, and the threshold of the underworld. She walks along the roadways and counsels the living and the dead. She is ancient, complex, and complicated.

Of all the Greek goddesses, Hecate alone could grant or refuse anything asked by mortals. She is the Queen of the Night, and those who seek her protection can move safely in the darkness. She is generous to her supplicants and is the voice of wisdom, divination, and dreams. Her link with the toad (!) symbolizes fertility and her help in childbirth. The knife she carries can cut an umbilical cord or the silver thread of life. Her totem is the crow, but also the owl.

She was so powerful that she was vilified with malice by the early Roman Church and many practices of evil have been attributed to her, the worst occurring during the Burning Times. In triple guise with Demeter and Persephone, she was the doorkeeper at Eleusis, the most famous of Greek mystery schools. However, at the school she did not take the role of the Crone, but of the Maiden. It is only by the Middle Ages that she fully assumed the guise of the Hag.

It began in Roman times where she was linked with Artemis, appearing as the Crone in the Moon Goddess trilogy. There is evidence to suggest early links with Brigid, the Celtic Triple Goddess. Some even deduce from old records that the goddesses divided the year between them, with Brigid ruling the long, sun-drenched days and

Hecate ruling the darkened half of the long nights.

Hecate is also complete as a Triple Goddess showing all three guises. The concept of the Great Goddess as a Triple Goddess dates back to ancient times. There is a young woman (Maiden), a birth-giving matron (Mother), and an old woman (Crone). Of course, these attributes were also ascribed to phases of the Moon. The Maiden is the first quarter, the Mother is the Full Moon, and the Crone is the waning third quarter.

The Maiden aspect represents the feminine principle. She is innocent in many ways, but she is also a seductress, confident in her sexuality and her sexual powers. However innocent, this guise does not imply virginity. The Maiden symbolizes enchantment, the promise of new beginnings, youth, and excitement. Her color is the white of purity.

The Mother is the Empress card—ripe, fertile, steadfast, and at the peak of her womanly powers. She is the female power principle in full glory, well able to rock the cradle while hunting like a lioness for food. She will fight to the death to protect her offspring. Her color is the red of passion.

The Crone reflects accumulated wisdom, compassion, healing, childbirth skills, old age, and experience. She mentors the Mother, who mentors the Maiden. She is the gateway to death, but also the guide to rebirth. It is her image and power that the male patriarchy has maligned as a threat to their stranglehold on power and wealth. Her traditional color is black.

Many mythologies worldwide have embraced the Triple Goddess concept. While many goddesses are a single aspect of this trilogy, it is entire and complete with Brigid of Ireland, the Greek Hecate, and Kali of India. The Morrigan is of Welsh legend, but the Vikings had the Norns, the Romans had the Fortunae, and the Druid priests had Diana Triformis, whom they borrowed and adapted from the Romans.

Triple Goddesses reach back directly to megalithic times and the cult of the Mothers. We see this dark lineage expressed in the guises of ecstasy in battle and of rebirth. Later versions evolved with them maintaining the sphere of warfare and using magic and incantation to defeat their enemies, which their chroniclers found both fierce and erotic.

The Celts give these goddesses the raven (battleground scavenger) and crow (creativity), while the Greeks offer the toad, and the Egyptians provide the frog, animal protectors of childbirth. Celtic Brigid is a fire goddess and a patroness of craftsmen and other creative arts.

All the Triple Goddesses are associated with the snake (psychic authority and death) and with the apple, the most magical of fruits. Hecate is the keeper of the triple crossroads (not just ordinary double ones) and director of the path for the dead in crossing the River Styx.

Because Hecate carries the torch through the dark half of the year, the dark night before any New Moon is appropriate for her rituals. As a "torch-bearing deity," she is a nocturnal goddess of the Moon.

Of course, Samhain is Hecate's festival, but sunset on November 16 marks the beginning of the Night of Hecate, which is often the night of initiation into her mysteries. Celebrate the powers of the dark feminine principle. Offer honey cakes and eggs to honor her. Light a new fire on the cleaned hearth or in your cauldron.

You can indulge in wearing and decorating with "witchy" black. However, the Celts traditionally wore "Druidic" white to welcome the first day of winter and the increasing darkness. It marks the descent into that darkness from which all new life and ideas come.

At traditional Samhain, a ritual at midnight on October 31 can bring a third quarter Moon in Leo. Check the time (and time zones) carefully to ensure that the Moon has moved into this fixed fire sign from the void-of-course Moon in Cancer. On November 7, which is astrological Samhain with the Sun at 15 degrees of Scorpio, the balsamic Moon is flirting tiredly in Libra. The New Year begins, according to the Celtic calendar, at sunset on the night before. Hecate's Night brings a first quarter Moon in Aquarius.

Fill a bowl of water as a symbol of the River Styx. Light candles to float in it for departed loved ones. Reflect on those who have crossed over. Honor them with a carved pumpkin. Burn black candles. Bring all your mojo to the altar to recharge. This is a potent time for prophecy and omens.

Any incense should help calm the mind so you can go within for divination. Use a blend of druidic herbs: mullein leaf, inula, propolis, juniper berries, sage, pine needles, elderberry pith, and/or sweet grass. Give your incense sustaining power with pine pitch, frankincense, or myrrh equal to the amount of dry herbs. Throw pinches on your fire, in your cauldron, or on the hearth.

Give honor to the Triple Goddess with offerings of roasted apple and cider. Decorate the altar with the fruits of the fall harvest. Prop your broom against it. Bob for sacred apples, a source of great magic, to commemorate the trip by water to Avalon.

Decorate little round cakes with lit miniature torches for Hecate's Night. They are the temple honey cakes found in all ancient ceremonies. Honey is sacred to Hecate.

Offered to the deities in most temples, honey cakes were often oval. When offered to Hecate and Artemis, the torch-bearing Goddesses of the Night, these cakes (called amphiphon, which can mean "shining by double light") were formed into little round circles and surrounded by lit miniature torches.

These honey cakes traveled well because they were flat, hard, dry biscuits that were often soaked in honey to soften them. Flavorless alone, the honey gave the cakes flavor and restorative powers to the hungry and weary traveler. It was the Arabs who gave them a more delicate texture and added almonds, wine, oranges, and sweet spices.

The following recipe is fairly simple, much lighter than the dense, hard cake of ancient times. It dates to the late 1800s and is probably Irish or English, as it calls for caster sugar. Arrange on a fireproof platter and affix lighted birthday candles in and around them.

Honey Cakes

1 stick butter	2 egg yolks
4 cups flour	1 egg white
¼ tsp. salt	1 cup milk
Grated rind of one orange	3 tbs. superfine sugar
1½ tsp. baking powder	2 tbs. honey

Cut the butter into the flour, salt, orange zest, and baking powder. Beat the two egg yolks and one egg white with the milk. Heat sugar and honey, stirring until well mixed. Stir wet ingredients into the dry mixture and turn out on a floured board. Roll lightly to ½-inch thickness. Cut out 2-inch rounds or ovals. Place on a greased baking sheet and bake in an oven preheated to 400 degrees F for 20 minutes. Remove to a rack and reduce oven heat to 250 degrees F. Pour topping (one cup of flavorful honey) over the hot cakes and sprinkle three tablespoons of ground, blanched almonds. Place rack of cakes in the cooler oven for 5 minutes, or until set.

Tips for the Busy Witch
by Emely Flak

A big part of Wicca is performing rituals, raising magical energy, and creating spells. This can be a challenge for time-poor Witches who may appreciate hints to make their path easier to follow. Every busy Witch needs spells on the run. Although this is usually a challenge to a new practitioner, even a proficient Witch may find that the creativity required for spell construction and ritual design is difficult to summon.

Most rituals require planning to ensure that each item is available and prepared appropriately. An elaborate ritual is like a work of theater, as the multisensory atmosphere largely contributes to the creation of magical and sacred space. In a coven, most members carefully prepare to check that they understand their respective roles. Along with time and place, set like a stage, every Witch—whether part of a coven or solitary—needs her ritual tools as props, her costume, and her "lines." The "lines," or the written spell, form just one dimension of a ritual.

Although there is nothing wrong with using prewritten spells from books or from the Internet, it's rewarding to create your own to help manifest your desires. There may be times you can't find the right spell for your unique situation. There's nothing like a spell or chant crafted by yourself to empower the words and personalize the experience. But writing a spell on short notice can be a daunting task for any Witch. The good news is that it can be painless and it becomes easier with practice. In fact, crafting your spell into a magical work of prose can be fun!

There are numerous magical correspondences to take into account to enhance our magic, such as Moon phase, day of the week, astrological and planetary influences, deities, herbs, color, oils, and incense. This part of spell planning can be relatively easy. There is a plethora of resources in print and on the Internet that help us identify the right energies to align with our specific intent. Nearly every introductory book and website on Wicca 101 details these correspondences. Keep these lists as a reference or at the back of your Book of Shadows. When short on time, they will be a useful resource to help your work align with natural energies. For many of us, the more difficult part of spell creation is writing the words.

The Magic Words

The three key considerations to take into account when writing lines for a spell are the purpose, the rhyme, and the intent.

In identifying the purpose of the spell, be specific with your wishes. Make sure the words clearly communicate your intent. This sounds simple, but we've all heard stories of spells that take a twist because the intent was unclear. For example, a spell to attract a lover who loves you unconditionally could result in a suffocating relationship. A spell wishing for a financial windfall could mean you receive money as the result of another's misfortune. This cautionary tale is a great example of the importance of being specific:

A couple had been married for twenty-five years and had just celebrated their sixtieth birthdays. During the celebration, a fairy appeared and said that because they had been a loving couple for many years, she would give them one wish each.

The wife wanted to travel with her husband around the world and the fairy waved her wand to produce two airline tickets.

It was the husband's turn. He paused for a moment and said, "I'd like to have a woman who is thirty years younger than I." The fairy picked up her wand to work her magic and made him 90 years old!

The moral of this story is be careful of what you wish for—and be precise about your desire, or the deities will cast their own interpretation.

There is an expectation that a spell will rhyme. Two lines in the Wiccan Rede are dedicated to this:

To bind the spell well every time
Let the spell be said in rhyme.

Rhyme generates the energy required to optimize the magic. When you are stuck on finding the right words, visit websites that are dedicated to finding the right ones to complement your rhyming lines. Some websites that allow you to type in a word and return a list of rhyming matches are www.rhymezone.com, www.rhyme.lycos.com, and www.poemzone.com.

These are invaluable resources for helping budding poets and creative Witches find rhyming words for their written craft. I found a book in a secondhand store written for songwriters that has becomes an invaluable resource packed with matching and rhyming words.

Producing rhyme flexes your creative muscles and helps you remember your lines. But be warned: a flash of inspiration finds you when you least expect it! Carry a notepad with you everywhere. I have had the "creative fairy" visit me with the perfect magical words in the middle of meetings, whilst watching a football match, in the shower, and when dining out.

Remember your obligation to practice responsible magic every time. Every spell must be pure and positive in its intent. This is the Law of Cause and Effect that relates to a key Wiccan ethical principle of "harm ye none, do what you will." That means no harm is intended in any magical word. Finish your spell with the words "and no harm

done, so mote it be" or a similar form of closure to confirm its positive purpose. Closely examine each word you have chosen and the significance of its associated action. Ensure that your invocation is specific and clear. Ask yourself the following:

Can it backfire? If it does, what are the consequences? Does it wish harm on anyone? Does it interfere with the free will of another?

Emergency Spells

There are times when a challenging situation occurs quite quickly and you need to carry out emergency magic for your immediate protection. There's no time to collect ritual tools, write spells, and wait for the right Moon phase. Don't underestimate the power of visualization. If you need to perform contingency magic and wish to craft a spell quite quickly, you can recall a simple, all-purpose spell, visualize the symbolism you need (such as a protective goddess or white light) and repeat to yourself like a mantra to raise the energy. Here is a simple one I wrote with my daughter to help her visualize protection from school bullies:

> *All the energy you send to me*
> *Will be returned to you times three.*

This short spell has served as a useful backup in many stressful situations for myself as well as my daughter. I often use it at work.

Gaining Confidence

Don't be turned off by prewritten spells. In fact, reading them will help you collect ideas on how to use rhyme and structure and how spells are closed. If you need to change a spell to better suit your needs, don't feel guilty. Changing spells will build your confidence for writing new ones.

Start off by keeping it simple. If the spell is too long to remember, recite it from a written document. If you are writing it by hand into your Book of Shadows, don't forget to include color. Make use of different colored pens to match the energy you want to raise or attract. For a love spell, use a red pen. For a healing spell, I write with a blue pen.

Remember to record all aspects of your magical work in your Book of Shadows (BOS). Your BOS (or Disk of Shadows, if you are totally techno-Pagan) is not only a record of your ritual work, it's a reflective learning tool to give you inspiration and confidence for your next round of spells. Assess what went well and what parts of the ritual can be improved. This makes your path an ongoing learning journey.

There will be times when a prewritten spell suits your purpose or requires only minor adjustments. On other occasions, you will need something unique. Tailor-made spells and rituals are intensely personal because they are imbued with your specific intent and energy. Even with a busy lifestyle, it's worth taking the time to master the skill of spell-crafting so you can create customized solutions for yourself.

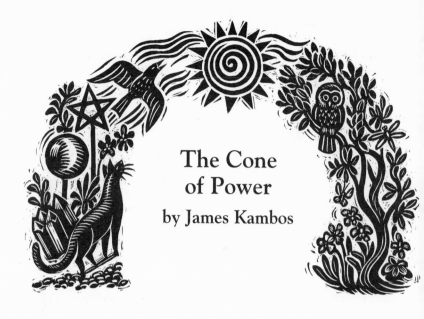

The Cone of Power

by James Kambos

The human body contains a great deal of psychic power and energy. It is this power that magical people draw upon when performing any magical work. Card reading, working a pendulum, scrying, and spell-casting are just a few examples of magical activities that require focusing our energy on a specific desired goal.

When magical energy is raised by a group of individuals working toward a common positive outcome, and within the sacred space of a magic circle, the psychic energy released is known as "raising the cone of power." When a group or coven concentrates on a specific magical goal and wills their objective to physically manifest itself, the results can be awesome.

Magical energy raised in this manner is called a cone of power because the force is visualized as a cone rising from the outer edge of the magic circle. As it rises, the group members visualize the energy peaking, or coming to a point, above the center of the circle. At this time each person releases their energy and lets the cone of power go. In their mind's eye, they see the cone of power flying through the unseen realm to its geographic destination. The cone of power can be used to attract any positive need into your life—protection, health, prosperity, a new home—or anything else you may desire.

A History of the Cone of Power

The act of raising a cone of power is one of the oldest magical rituals known to the human race. In fact, the cone of power concept was already ancient before the great empires of Egypt, Greece, or Rome ever existed.

Stone-age cave art discovered in Spain supports this theory. Some early primitive cave art found in northern Spain depicts women dancing around the nude figure of a man. The women are wearing pointed Witch-style hats (a cone of power symbol), and appear to be raising magical energy. The nude male figure in the center may represent a spiritual leader. Or, he may symbolize the Hunter—the life-giving provider which the ancient clan depended upon for food. Considering this, we could conclude that the dancers are raising a protective cone of energy to attract a bountiful food supply.

Pre-Columbian Mexican art has also been found depicting Witch figures wearing pointed hats, indicating that the magical cone shape was also known in ancient North America since early times.

One of the most enduring rituals in history, which echoes many of the same basic elements as the cone of power, is the 700-year-old traditional dance performed by the Whirling Dervishes of Turkey. This sacred dance or rite was created by the great poet and mystic, Mevlana Celaleddin Rumi. The ritual dance is still performed by the Whirling Dervish Order. And, although the rite is not identical to raising a cone of power, there are some fascinating similarities.

The dance is also performed in a circle, and, like the dancers in the magic circle, the dervishes achieve an altered state of awareness. The white skirts worn by the dancers flow outward as they spin and resemble the sacred cone shape. The tall hats worn by each dervish are not pointed, but do allude to the shape of the ancient wizard's hat. And the mystical energy raised during the whirling is achieved by chanting, music, and movement—methods also found in building a cone of power.

Throughout history the cone of power has been used to raise a shield of protective energy, just one of its many uses. Perhaps the most poignant example of this took place in

England during World War II. It was 1940. Nazi forces had already invaded Belgium, Luxembourg, and the Netherlands. In June of that year, France surrendered to Germany. Fear swept through England that a Nazi invasion was imminent.

So, on August 1, 1940 (Lammas), covens from southern England gathered in the New Forest region to raise a cone of power which would protect their nation against the Nazi armies. Among the Witches in attendance was the famous occultist, Gerald Gardner. This was one of the greatest rites in modern Witchcraft. So strong was the determination to repel the evil Nazi forces that the extraordinary ritual was performed four times.

Collectively, the covens attempted to send out a psychic message to the Nazis that they would fail if they tried to invade. The purpose of this ritual was not only to build a protective shield, but to affect the decision-making process of the Nazi High Command.

As it turned out, the Nazis did not invade England. And we will never know for sure if the Lammas Day rite had anything to do with this outcome. But, this was one of the Craft's finest moments, and is an excellent example of how the cone of power can be used for "the good of all."

How to Raise a Cone of Power

Here is one example of how a cone of power can be raised.

Before casting a magic circle, the group/coven must decide on a specific magical goal and for whom the rite will be performed. As discussed earlier, the goal may be any positive need—good health, prosperity, romance, peace, etc. The ritual may also be performed for an individual, group, community, or even our planet. After deciding these things, you must also decide how the power will be raised. This can be done through meditation, chanting, dancing, music, or a combination of these methods.

Once the group has decided on what to do, cast the circle according to your tradition. In the center of the circle you might wish to place a photo or symbol of your objective. Or you could burn a candle, appropriate incense, and, if conditions permit, a bonfire.

Now let the magic begin. As the group begins concentrating on their goal, everyone should join hands. To set the tone, the group may say something in unison such as, "hand to hand; heart to heart. Let the power start."

If a musical instrument such as a drum or flute is used, now would be a good time to start. The traditional Round Dance, if it will be used to raise the cone of power, may begin now. The dance should move in a clockwise (deosil) direction. Allow the dancers to wear loose, comfortable garments to aid the flow of energy. As the power heightens, the dancers should increase their speed. Everyone should continue holding hands and keep visualizing the agreed upon magical goal.

When the movement within the circle peaks, you may feel an altered state of awareness. The group leader will give the direction to release the power. At this moment, the dancing usually stops.

Now the group should raise their arms. The energy will feel as if it is coming up from the earth, rising through each person, until it is released through the fingertips or head. Visualize the goal in its completed form.

The power will be raised first from the perimeter of the circle, then it will rise above the center of the circle, where it will form a peak. This is the cone of power.

Through the magical willpower of the group, the cone of power is released into the realm of spirit, and on to its final destination. True psychics who have taken part in cone of power rituals say the cone appears as a blue-white light.

After the ritual, which can be exhausting, the circle should be closed and released. Everyone should relax; light refreshments may be served. And, positive conversation about the outcome of the ritual is encouraged. Leave the group knowing that your request will physically manifest itself in the most perfect way.

The Cone of Power and Magical Symbolism

We now know that the cone shape is an ancient and universal magical symbol. It has deep mystical significance.

As I've said, the Witches' pointed hat is a cone symbol. But the cone is also associated with the circle, as well as eternity. Since its shape is a triangle, it is magically linked to the number three and to

the three aspects of the life cycle: birth, death, and rebirth.

It is no coincidence that the ancient civilizations of Egypt and Mexico built their great monuments in the form of pyramids. They also must have known the significance of the cone shape.

In magic, the cone is a symbol of our highest aspirations and spiritual goals. It is our link to the divine.

A Cone of Power Charm

Since the cone is one of the most ancient and magical of all symbols, here is a simple charm you can create to invoke the mystical energy of the cone.

Upon a sheet of clean white paper, draw a triangle with three equal sides. Beneath the base of the triangle write the name of the ancient Mother Goddess, Astarte. She was considered a warrior and a creator. The cone was one of her sacred symbols.

Within the triangle write your wish. When you feel the time is right—next week, next month, or next year—burn your wish in a ritual fire. And, like the cone of power, may your wish soar to the Heavens. So mote it be.

For Further Reading

Buckland, Raymond. *Buckland's Complete Book of Witchcraft*. St. Paul, MN: Llewellyn, 1988.

Valiente, Doreen. *Witchcraft For Tomorrow*. Custer, WA: Phoenix, 1978.

Weinstein, Marion. *Earth Magic: A Dianic Book of Shadows*. Custer, WA: Phoenix, 1980.

My Other Broomstick

by Dallas Jennifer Cobb

Wrap yourself in your magical garb, gather your sacred tools, and get going. Whether you are off to a ritual, community gathering, or sacred circle, you have to get there somehow. While broomstick may be your vehicle of choice, these days most of us use automobiles.

Even if you are traveling in a mundane piece of metal, you can imbue your vehicle with magical intention—banish unwanted energy, bless the vehicle to instill the power and protection of the gods and goddesses, and cast a protective spell around the vehicle.

We all spend a good deal of time in vehicles as drivers and passengers. With the rise in incidents of road rage and vehicular aggression, many Pagans practice magic while in the car and on the move. Spiritual and psychic protection can minimize common concerns and positively influence conditions and situations that arise while traveling.

Included are some ideas to help you to magically bless your other broomstick.

Cleansing Your Other Broomstick

Cleansing, or banishing, is done to remove old, unwanted energy. Whether you drive a new or used car, it is good to conduct a regular cleansing to remove energetic accumulation. Generally, the elements of earth, air, fire, and water are used to cleanse. With a vehicle, you could mindfully wash your car (water), wipe it dry (air), admire it in

19

the sunlight (fire), and check the tires (your vehicle's connection with the earth).

As you do this, consciously cleanse the vehicle of any old unwanted energy it may still hold, asking the elements to take it away and neutralize it.

Blessing Your Other Broomstick

A blessing usually follows a cleansing and instills the vehicle with the power and protection of the gods and goddesses, imbuing it with positive, magical energy.

Blessings can be done after the regular cleansing, and every time that you get into the vehicle. It is possible to anoint your vehicle with essential oils from herbs having magical protection qualities such as comfrey root and mint. Or, you can make up your own protection spell for regular use in combination with a blessing.

As I buckle my daughter into her booster seat, I envision protective white light surrounding her. For good measure, I always kiss her before closing the door. Walking around to the driver's side, I envision a larger orb surrounding the car, invoking protection.

Sliding into my seat, I place both hands on the dashboard and utter out loud: "I bless this car with love and light." Reaching up for the shoulder belt, I envision the protective light surrounding me as I do up the buckle.

Make protection blessings a regular part of getting into your vehicle, and instill this magic as a regular practice. Let it become part of what you do, every day, every drive.

A quick ritual such as this serves two purposes: it helps us to pause, take note and become focused and fully present to the task of driving,

and it invokes good energy around us, making negative interactions less likely. When we hold a negative charge, we are far more likely to attract negative energy to us than if we hold a positive charge.

So take a moment, bless yourself and bless your broomstick. Then move consciously and deliberately into the operation of your vehicle before every trip.

Blessing the Journey

In addition to protective blessings of the vehicle and passengers, you can bless the journey. Petition the gods and goddesses to watch over your excursion. Visualize yourself arriving safely at your destination. And later, when you do arrive, give thanks to the gods and goddesses.

Or call in the elements, invoking their powers. Make up your own invocation, or borrow mine:

Earth, air, fire, water,
please protect me and my daughter.

The simple task of chanting, incanting, influences our energy and elevates our spirit.

Auto Altars to Go

Create a small sacred space in your vehicle to keep your magical objects. If you are traveling in someone else's car you may have to satisfy yourself with keeping the sacred objects in your pocket or pack.

One of the most common forms of protection is the talisman. People from many spiritual practices carry talismans, an image of a protector, or a sacred object or item. Whether you have a large sticker with a protective maternal face affixed to the dashboard, a Happy Face ball smiling merrily on the antenna, or crystals covertly sitting in the glove compartment, these objects can be imbued with the energy of protective safety, and carried with you throughout your journey.

Many crystals and minerals are known for their protective powers. Those crystals and minerals that are dark in color, like smoky quartz, jet quartz, bloodstone, moonstone, and garnet, are thought to make you less visible to hostile people.

If you have children, consider which simple toys can be charged with energy. An angel affixed to the window, a protective mama bear dangling over the car seat, or a bunny ballerina with a crystal hoop hanging from the rearview mirror can be charged with the tasks of magical protection.

To the untrained eye, the sacred objects will appear mundane, not magical. They may seem interesting, but will rarely draw attention or raise questions. These are your personal magic talismans.

Whatever objects you choose as protective talismans, take the time to charge them, imbuing them with magical power. Tell them what you want of them, what their work will be in the world, and thank them and bless them for what they do.

Divine Protection

In many cultures and faiths, sacred deities and saints are used as talismans to invoke safe travel. Catholics call upon St. Christopher and often place small plastic statues on their dashboards. There are cards printed with the image of St. Christopher on one side and The Motorist's Prayer on the other, asking for protection of the car and other pedestrians and vehicles.

The Tibetan Buddhist symbol Kalachakra hangs in many Mongolian taxis. Usually placed on the rearview mirror, it protects against accidents.

The protective goddess Kwan Yin is invoked in urban China. She is said to protect both the vehicle and its occupants from accidents, and to keep pedestrians and animals from being hit.

Motorist Magic

Driving requires attention and concentration. All of our senses must be employed in the operation of the vehicle. The following magic should only be performed while you are fully alert to your surroundings, and operating your vehicle in a safe and responsible manner.

Make motorist magic your ally. Some simple magical practices, sometimes known as common courtesy, can transform a tense and volatile situation.

Make a habit of being a courteous driver. More than operating your vehicle in a calm and safe manner, courtesy includes allowing other vehicles and pedestrians to proceed ahead of you. When you come to a traffic snarl that vehicles are attempting to squeeze through, invoke grace and generosity, and wave that other vehicle on ahead of you. The ten seconds that you pause to allow someone else to proceed

won't really affect your journey negatively, but the small positive charge of the interaction may just uplift you and the other driver, changing the nature of your day.

Let go of the energy of rush and importance. Use your breath to let go of worry and negative charge. Inhale calm and grace, exhale worry and aggression. Just blow it out, blow it all away, let it go. Minimizing the negative charge that you hold will limit the negative energy that comes your way.

But if you encounter someone who honks their horn or gesticulates wildly at you, practice the art of magical transformation. Make eye contact if you can safely do so, smile and wave, and mouth the words "thank you." Then move on.

Petitioning for Parking

In large urban areas, parking can be difficult and frustrating. But there are ways to influence the fates by petitioning the Parking Goddess. Start well before you arrive at your destination. In your mind's eye, envision the street. Even if you have never been there before, envision the usual setup of parking spaces and meters. See the cars inhabiting those spaces, and begin invoking the magical flow of time and energy. Envision one of those cars leaving the space just as you arrive.

Ask the Parking Goddess to help you:

Be with me now, as I find a space, I know that everything has a place.

And, as you arrive at your destination, look for people entering their cars, or cars preparing to leave. While it may take a few minutes, remember: in the magical world, there is flow. And flow makes everything possible. Even parking spaces.

In her book, *Everyday Magic,* Dorothy Morrison has a short but effective parking spell:

Goddess, Mother, lift Your face and find for me a parking space.

And if you lose your car in a large parking lot, you can use your magic keypad device (that's the little red button marked Panic) to locate your car, or try Dorothy Morrison's invocation:

Ancients, come from near and far, find for me my waiting car.

For Further Reading
Morrison, Dorothy. *Everyday Magic: Spells and Rituals for Modern Living.* St. Paul, MN: Llewellyn, 1998.

Making Magical Inks
by Lynn Smythe

Practitioners of the ancient occult arts once thought that using animal blood as part of their rituals would add extra power to their magical workings. Modern Pagans, magicians, and Witches are in tune with nature and strive to live in harmony with all of Mother Earth's creatures. Botanical substitutes for the animal blood are now available for use by ethical practitioners of the magical arts. Magical inks can be used to write out your talismans or Book of Shadows entries along with writing implements such as a metal nib calligraphy pen, a feather quill, a glass dip pen, or even a small, thin artist's paint brush.

Dragon's blood comes from the resin—that is, the sap—of certain types of plants. Dragon's blood resin is used to produce three types of magical inks: dragon's blood ink, dove's blood ink, and bat's blood ink. No animal products are used. While you can purchase these inks from a variety of new age and metaphysical stores, making your own inks can add additional strength and authenticity to your own spells, talismans, and Book of Shadows entries.

Botanical Origins

Dragon's blood resin is produced from a variety of plants, which can be found in parts of Asia such as China, Malaysia, and Sumatra. The versatile resin was once used as a varnish by furniture-makers in the eighteenth century. As a medicinal herb, dragon's blood was once used externally to help heal wounds.

Dracaena draco—a.k.a. dragon tree or Canary Island dragon's blood. A member of the agave family, its resin is collected by damaging the bark and collecting the sap.

Dracaena cinnabari—a.k.a. Socotrine dragon's blood. Another plant in the agave family that produces resin from its damaged bark.

Daemonorops draco—a.k.a. Calamus draco or dragon's blood

palm. This plant, a type of palm tree, is the most commonly harvested to produce dragon's blood resin, which is collected from its immature, cherry-size fruits. Other plants which have at one time been harvested to produce dragon's blood resin include Croton draco, or Mexican dragon's blood; Pterocarpus draco, or Guadaloupe dragon's blood; and Dracaena terminalis, or Chinese dragon's blood.

The resin produced from all of these plants dries to a hard and shiny, reddish-brown material which fractures easily. Although dragon's blood is available as chunks of resin, it is easier to use if you purchase it in powder form. It isn't the easiest process to grind the chunks into a fine powder using a mortar and pestle, And it can also be quite messy to grind your own powder.

The Powers

Dragon's blood is a masculine plant attributed to the planet Mars, the deity Ares, and the element fire. Often used in ritualistic work to exploit its magical powers of love, protection, exorcism, strength, and purification, dragon's blood is also a powerful incense to burn when consecrating your magical tools—simply pass each tool through the smoke the resin produces as it burns on a smoldering charcoal disc. If you utilize tarot cards in your magical workings, dragon's blood is an herb that can help with your interpretations—especially when reflecting on the meanings of either the Lovers card or the Emperor card.

Authentic dragon's blood ink, which is a dark, orange-red color, is commonly used to seal and protect spells and rituals. Adding dragon's blood to magical spells and talismans helps increase their potency. The magical and metaphysical properties associated with dragon's blood include courage, power, protection, and spirituality. It can be used when astral traveling to offer protection on the astral plane and to produce psychic insight.

As the dove is sacred to Venus, the goddess of love, dove's blood ink is used for writing out love letters and spells along with relationship petitions. This ink can also be used when creating prosperity and abundance amulets and talismans. Additional magical and metaphysical properties associated with dove's blood include fertility, fidelity, peace, reconciliation, romance, and tranquility.

Bat's blood ink is used for havoc, hexing, binding, cursing, revenge, and destruction spells. In a more positive light, bat's blood, and its associations of decreasing and diminishing, can be used to write a spell to help rid yourself of a bad habit or to banish any evil entities in your home. Additional magical and metaphysical properties associated with bat's blood include discord, separation, and tension.

The Recipes

Dragon's blood resin is not soluble in water. However, it is soluble in a high proof alcohol, so use an alcohol base when making these magical inks. I recommend using isopropyl alcohol, which is 91 percent alcohol by volume. Isopropyl rubbing alcohol, 70 percent alcohol by volume, can also be used, but the dragon's blood resin will take longer to dissolve. Both varieties are available at your local pharmacy. Alcohol is also a preservative, so these inks may be stored at room temperature.

Make a large batch of the base ink, which gives you dragon's blood ink. Dove's blood and bat's blood ink can be easily made by adding certain essential oils to the basic formula of dragon's blood ink. The color of these homemade magical inks will be a pale to medium orange.

I purchased my ingredients for making magical inks from a wholesale botanical supplier. My package of dragon's blood resin came in a one-pound package which was in the form of two large resin balls, each weighing approximately eight ounces. As these balls were both too large to fit into my mortar and pestle, I had to initially pound them to a smaller size. I placed the resin balls on a thick layer of newspaper on top of my butcher-block kitchen island. Then I used my pestle to break each ball into pieces that would fit inside of my mortar. Then I added one of the smaller pieces to my mortar and continued to pound and grind down the resin until it was mostly a fine powder with some small lumps. I stored the excess large pieces in a glass container.

Dragon's Blood Ink

2 tbs. powdered dragon's
    blood resin
1 cup isopropyl alcohol

Place the powdered resin in the bottom of a one-pint canning jar. Top off with the alcohol and cover with the lid. Shake the jar once a day for up to one week. Strain out and discard the resin by placing a paper towel or coffee filter inside a mesh strainer, which is placed over a clean container. At this point you have dragon's blood ink. To make dove's blood or bat's blood ink, stir in the appropriate essential oils as listed below. Store the finished inks in individual dark amber glass bottles with a screw-on lid.

Bat's Blood Ink

  1 ounce dragon's blood ink
10 drops German chamomile essential oil
10 drops myrrh essential oil
10 drops cinnamon essential oil

German chamomile essential oil is a dark blue color and is used to combat curses and spells. Myrrh is associated with the powers of protection, exorcism, healing, and spirituality. Cinnamon has magical attributes similar to myrrh, namely spirituality, healing, and protection, along with the properties of success and power.

Dove's Blood Ink

1 ounce dragon's blood ink
10 drops cinnamon essential oil
10 drops bay essential oil
10 drops rose essential oil

Cinnamon is also credited with the properties of love and lust and is associated with the love goddess Venus. Roses are a terrific ingredient to use to create effective love spells. Bay is associated with the property of helping love to stay strong.

January

1 Monday
2nd ♊
Color: Gray

Kwanzaa ends
New Year's Day
Birthday of Sir James Frazer,
author of *The Golden Bough*, 1854

2 Tuesday
2nd ♊
☽ v/c 5:06 am
☽ enters ♋ 10:14 am
Color: Red

If you dream of an antique shop, you may wish to connect
with your past, and you have choices ahead

☺ Wednesday
2nd ♋
☽ v/c 8:57 am
Full Moon 8:57 am
♀ enters ♒ 10:31 pm
Color: Yellow

Cold Moon
Death of Edgar Cayce, psychic, 1945

4 Thursday
3rd ♋
☽ enters ♌ 4:14 pm
Color: Green

Aquarian Tabernacle Church
registered in Australia by
Lady Tamara Von Forslun, 1994

5 Friday
3rd ♌
Color: White

The hearth is the heart of the home, and
hearth fires embody loyalty to family

Cold Moon

On the year's first Full Moon, also called the Wolf Moon, take time to reflect on the magic and medicine of the wolf. A popular animal ally with Witches and magic users, the wolf is a pathfinder, leader, and teacher. The wolf has an incredible sense of family, but also independence. The wolf encourages the teacher in us to share our knowledge. Perform a spell to tap your inner wisdom. Whether sharing your knowledge with circle or coven mates or teaching a formal class, calling on the wolf will give you the strength to walk your individual magical path and help others find theirs.

Set up your altar with white candles and a representation (small statue, photo) of the wolf. As the Full Moon rises, face the Moon, and call upon the wolf's magic. When ready, repeat the spell below three times.

On this enchanted night of the full Wolf Moon,
Send wisdom to me, by this Witches' tune.
Ally and friend, I honor the Moon at which you bay,
Help me to teach and lead in the best possible way.

—Ellen Dugan

---

6 Saturday

3rd ♌
☽ v/c 7:55 pm
Color: Brown

Twelfth Night/Epiphany
Patricia Crowther's witchcraft
radio show, *A Spell of Witchcraft*,
airs in Britain, 1971

7 Sunday

3rd ♌
☽ enters ♍ 1:18 am
Color: Yellow

January

8 Monday
3rd ♍
Color: Lavender

Birthday of MacGregor Mathers,
one of the three original founders
of the Golden Dawn, 1854
Death of Dion Fortune, 1946

9 Tuesday
3rd ♍
☽ v/c 7:51 am
☽ enters ♎ 1:15 pm
Color: White

Jamie Dodge wins lawsuit against
the Salvation Army, which fired her
based on her Wiccan religion, 1989

10 Wednesday
3rd ♎
Color: Brown

◗ Thursday
3rd ♎
4th quarter 7:44 am
☽ v/c 8:56 pm
Color: Turquoise

12 Friday
4th ♎
☽ enters ♏ 2:08 am
Color: Pink

Mary Smith hanged in England;
she had quarreled with neighbors,
who said that the Devil appeared
to her as a black man, 1616

13 Saturday
4th ♏
Color: Gray

Final witchcraft laws
repealed in Austria, 1787

14 Sunday
4th ♏
☽ v/c 10:49 am
☽ enters ♐ 1:11 pm
Color: Orange

Official Confession of Error by
jurors of Salem Witch Trials, 1696

Human Be-In, a Pagan-style festival,
takes place in San Francisco, attended by
Timothy Leary and Allen Ginsburg, 1967

January

15 Monday

4th ♐
☿ enters ♒ 4:24 am
Color: White

Birthday of Martin Luther King, Jr. (observed)

16 Tuesday

4th ♐
♂ enters ♑ 3:54 pm
☽ v/c 4:28 pm
☽ enters ♑ 8:49 pm
Color: Black

Birthday of Dr. Dennis Carpenter,
Circle Sanctuary

17 Wednesday

4th ♑
Color: Topaz

In Babylonian tradition, heliotrope is the
stone of divination and invulnerability,
sacred to the gods

☽ Thursday

4th ♑
New Moon 11:01 pm
☽ v/c 11:01 pm
Color: Purple

19 Friday

1st ♑
☽ enters ♒ 1:15 am
Color: Rose

Birthday of Dorothy Clutterbuck,
who initiated Gerald Gardner, 1880

Set in Eastern Standard Time (EST)

Omio Yemaya

We praise a woman
  Ancient ancestress
We praise a goddess
  Mighty Yemaya
We praise a dancer
  Who flows like oceans
We praise a helper
  Who has known trouble
We praise a priestess
  She who knows magic
We praise an elder
  She who remembers
We praise a woman
  Mother of millions
We praise a goddess
  Hear us, Yemaya!
              —Elizabeth Barrette

Written in the style of an African praise poem

---

20 Saturday

1st ≈
☉ enters ≈ 6:01 am
Color: Blue

Islamic New Year
Sun enters Aquarius

---

21 Sunday

1st ≈
☽ v/c 12:00 am
☽ enters ♓ 3:48 am
Color: Gold

Celtic Tree Month of Rowan begins

January

22 Monday
1st ♓
Color: Silver

In Greece, purple is the color of royalty,
secrecy, and divine mysteries

23 Tuesday
1st ♓
☽ v/c 2:11 am
☽ enters ♈ 5:52 am
Color: Gray

Geodes look like plain rocks on the outside,
but crystals line their hollow interiors
—perfect for childbearing spells

24 Wednesday
1st ♈
Color: White

◐ Thursday
1st ♈
☽ v/c 4:50 am
☽ enters ♉ 8:28 am
2nd quarter 6:01 pm
Color: Crimson

Birthday of Robert Burns, Scottish poet, 1759

26 Friday
2nd ♉
Color: Coral

Quickening Moon

The Full Moon in February falls on Imbolc, an ancient festival of light honoring the sacred Mother. Tap into the power surge of two magical days in one. Candles feature prominently into this holiday as do the seasonal symbols: snow and ice as well as flowers like white snowdrops and purple crocus. The Full Moon at Imbolc is a time of purification and illumination—a perfect occasion to purge old habits and start fresh.

This indoor ritual requires a white and a purple candle, a bowl, and a cup of snow or chopped ice. Place the candles on either side of the bowl, light them, and then repeat the spell:

This is the Sabbat of Imbolc, and the Moon is round,
I cast away old habits, never more to be found.
This melting ice/snow represents the things I release,
Goddess bless me in this season of light and peace.

Once the snow/ice melts, pour it down the drain. Then brush off your hands and say goodbye to those bad habits and hello to new possibilities.

—Ellen Dugan

---

27 Saturday

2nd ♉
☽ v/c 11:08 am
☽ enters ♊ 12:10 pm
♀ enters ♓ 10:32 pm
Color: Indigo

---

28 Sunday

2nd ♊
Color: Amber

The sun embodies the active principle of
nature, including solar deities like
Ra (Egyptian), Loki (Scandinavian),
and Amaterasu (Japanese)

January/February

29 Monday
2nd ♊
☽ v/c 1:40 pm
☽ enters ♋ 5:16 pm
Color: Ivory

30 Tuesday
2nd ♋
☽ v/c 4:30 pm
Color: Maroon

Birthday of Zsuzsanna Budapest,
feminist Witch

31 Wednesday
2nd ♋
Color: Yellow

Dr. Fian, believed to be the head
of the North Berwick Witches, found
guilty and executed for witchcraft in
Scotland by personal order of King
James VI (James I of England), 1591

1 Thursday
2nd ♋
☽ enters ♌ 12:14 am
Color: White

☺ Friday
2nd ♌
Full Moon 12:45 am
☿ enters ♓ 4:20 am
Color: Purple

Imbolc
Groundhog Day
Quickening Moon
Leo Martello becomes a third-degree
Welsh traditionalist, 1973

Imbolc

Festival of Brigid and the element of fire, this sabbat is celebrated with bonfires, candles, and blazing cauldrons. A crossquarter day, Imbolc was originally an Irish celebration, which may have merged with Candlemas. All things sacred to Brigid and the growing light of the lengthening days have added power to this day. The celebrations also had conservative aspects, as winter supplies dwindled and preparations

for the coming spring planting were just beginning. Feasting is neither extravagant nor frivolous.

It is a time of water scrying and making offerings to the sacred waters for the new lives growing within their mothers' bellies. Mystical visions and creative inspirations come through easily at Imbolc. The blessings of Brigid are upon all who honor Her with sacred healing fire on this day.

The Goddess Brigid is the patroness of bards, poets, smiths, and healers, favoring them with Her gifts, skills, and wisdom—the bard and poet, the sparks of inspiration and imagination; the smith, the spark of the glowing forge; and the healer, the spark of energy balance and restoration.

—Abby Willowroot

---

3 Saturday

3rd ♌
☽ v/c 5:55 am
☽ enters ♍ 9:34 am
Color: Brown

The tortoise figures in both Chinese and Japanese culture as a symbol of longevity and divination

---

4 Sunday

3rd ♍
Color: Orange

Imbolc crossquarter day
(Sun reaches 15° Aquarius)

February

5 Monday
3rd ♍
☽ v/c 5:37 pm
☽ enters ♎ 9:15 pm
Color: Gray

The unicorn, a fabulous one-horned beast,
stands for virtue, purity,
beauty, prosperity, and peace

6 Tuesday
3rd ♎
Color: Red

7 Wednesday
3rd ♎
Color: White

Death of Thomas Aquinas, scholar who
wrote that heresy was a product of
ignorance and therefore criminal, and
who refuted the *Canon Episcopi,* 1274

8 Thursday
3rd ♎
☽ v/c 6:38 am
☽ enters ♏ 10:09 am
Color: Crimson

Birthday of Susun Weed, owner of
Wise Woman Publishing
Birthday of Evangeline Adams,
American astrologer, 1868

9 Friday
3rd ♏
⚶ enters ♐ 1:26 pm
Color: Rose

Cottage Cheese Pie

1½ cups graham cracker crumbs
   (about ⅓ of a 16 oz. package)
1 cup sugar, divided
4 to 6 tbs. melted butter
16 oz. (2 cups) cottage cheese (low fat
   works just fine)
3 eggs
1 tbs. lemon juice
1 tsp. vanilla extract
¼ tsp. salt
1 tbs. grated lemon rind (optional)

Preheat oven to 350 degrees F. Mix graham cracker crumbs (you may use a food processor or blender to crush the graham crackers) and ⅓ cup sugar. Add melted butter, mix, and press into pie plate, saving about 3 or 4 tablespoons for decoration, if desired.

Puree the cottage cheese in food processor, add ⅔ cup sugar, and blend. Then add eggs, lemon juice, vanilla extract, salt, and grated lemon rind. Whirl until blended and pour into pie plate. Decorate with reserved crumbs. Bake for 45 to 50 minutes at 350 degrees F. Cool thoroughly before serving. Refrigerate any leftovers.

—Magenta Griffith

☽ Saturday
3rd ♏
4th quarter 4:51 am
☽ v/c 5:39 am
☽ enters ♐ 10:01 pm
Color: Blue

Zsuzsanna Budapest arrested and later
convicted for fortunetelling, 1975

11 Sunday
4th ♐
Color: Amber

Wear red to enhance love, virility, and passion

February

12 Monday
4th ♐
Color: Lavender

Gerald Gardner, founder of the
Gardnerian tradition, dies
of heart failure, 1964

13 Tuesday
4th ♐
☽ v/c 3:45 am
☽ enters ♑ 6:42 am
☿ ℞ 11:38 pm
Color: White

*Wear carnelian to dissipate negative energies
such as apathy, jealousy, fear, or rage*

14 Wednesday
4th ♑
✳ ℞ 4:48 am
☽ v/c 10:24 pm
Color: Brown

Valentine's Day

Elsie Blum, a farmhand from
Oberstedten, Germany, sentenced
to death for witchcraft, 1652

15 Thursday
4th ♑
☽ enters ♒ 11:34 am
Color: Turquoise

Pope Leo X issues papal bull to ensure that
the secular courts carry out executions
of Witches convicted by the Inquisition,
1521; the bull was a response to the courts'
refusal to carry out the work of the Church

16 Friday
4th ♒
Color: Coral

☽ **Saturday**

4th ♒

New Moon 11:14 am

☽ v/c 11:14 am

☽ enters ♓ 1:30 pm

Color: Indigo

18 Sunday

1st ♓

☉ enters ♓ 8:09 pm

Color: Gold

Chinese New Year (boar)

Sun enters Pisces

Celtic Tree Month of Ash begins

February

19 Monday
1st ♓
☽ v/c 11:43 am
☽ enters ♈ 2:06 pm
Color: Silver

Presidents' Day (observed)

20 Tuesday
1st ♈
Color: Maroon

Mardi Gras
Society for Psychical Research,
devoted to paranormal research,
founded in London, 1882

21 Wednesday
1st ♈
♀ enters ♈ 3:21 am
☽ v/c 12:42 pm
☽ enters ♉ 3:03 pm
Color: Brown

Ash Wednesday
Birthday of Patricia Telesco,
Wiccan author
Stewart Farrar initiated into
Alexandrian Wicca, 1970
Death of Theodore Parker Mills, 1996

22 Thursday
1st ♉
Color: Green

Birthday of Sybil Leek, Wiccan author, 1922

23 Friday
1st ♉
☽ v/c 2:46 pm
☽ enters ♊ 5:42 pm
Color: Pink

Set in Eastern Standard Time (EST)

Dreampipe

Blow, blow the didgeridoo:
Hear the hopping kangaroo
And crested cassowary
Flightless and solitary
And brazen kookaburras
Like lost coloraturas.
Listen for sudden thunder:
Storms come quickly downunder
And the wind, willy-willy,
Tears down the waterlily.
Songlines reach to deliver
Their power like a river
All across Australia
Clad in rich regalia
That keeps alive history
Through magic and mystery—
Then vanished, silent, hidden,
Unremarked, overridden—
Till dreampipe and bullroarer
Summon the next explorer.

—Elizabeth Barrette

Written in the style of an Australian playabout poem

◐ Saturday

1st ♊
2nd Quarter 2:56 am
Color: Gray

Eat turnips to help release a bad
relationship that you've just ended

---

25 Sunday

2nd ♊
☽ v/c 8:21 pm
♂ enters ♒ 8:32 pm
☽ enters ♋ 10:47 pm
Color: Yellow

Clove oil enhances sexual attraction and grants
courage; wear it for success with the opposite sex

---

26 Monday
2nd ♋
☿ enters ≈ 10:00 pm
Color: Gray

27 Tuesday
2nd ♋
☽ v/c 1:03 am
Color: Black

Pope John XXII issues first papal bull
to discuss the practice of witchcraft, 1318

Birthday of Rudolf Steiner,
philosopher and father of the
biodynamic farming movement, 1861

28 Wednesday
2nd ♋
☽ enters ♌ 6:29 am
Color: Topaz

Dream of a wand, and you're dwelling on
your active, inner power;
what can you do to manifest your needs?

1 Thursday
2nd ♌
Color: Purple

Preliminary hearings in the
Salem Witch trials held, 1692
Birthday of the Golden Dawn, 1888
Covenant of the Goddess (COG) formed, 1975

2 Friday
2nd ♌
☽ v/c 2:02 pm
☽ enters ♍ 4:32 pm
Color: White

Storm Moon

The Full Moon in March heralds a total lunar eclipse, which will be visible across the eastern United States, Europe, Africa, and western Asia. During this mysterious time, as the Moon falls under the earth's shadow, magic abounds. Lunar enchantments are especially potent. Why? During the eclipse, the Moon appears to go through all of its phases in a matter of hours.

Tonight, while the Moon is covered with that dusky-burgundy shadow, work for transformation and to increase psychic abilities. To honor the lunar eclipse, light two small tapers, one white and the other burgundy or dusky brown. Sit and meditate on changes you'd like. Repeat this spell as the eclipse begins.

> As the Goddess pulls her soft cloak across the face of the Moon,
> I light a dark and white candle to bring transformation soon.
> As the eclipse shows all the lunar phases so bright,
> May my psychic talents be seen in a whole new light.

Once the spell is spoken, go find a good spot to watch one of nature's finest shows. Allow the candles to burn in a safe place until they go out.

—Ellen Dugan

☺ Saturday

2nd ♍
Full Moon 6:17 pm
Color: Blue

Storm Moon
Lunar eclipse 6:22 pm, 13° ♍ 00'

---

4 Sunday

3rd ♍
Color: Gold

Purim
Church of All Worlds incorporates in
Missouri, 1968, becoming the first Pagan
church to incorporate in the U.S.

March

5 Monday
3rd ♍
☽ v/c 1:56 am
☽ enters ♎ 4:25 am
Color: Lavender

6 Tuesday
3rd ♎
Color: White

Birthday of Laurie Cabot, Wiccan author

7 Wednesday
3rd ♎
☽ v/c 2:51 pm
☽ enters ♏ 5:16 pm
☿ D 11:44 pm
Color: Yellow

William Butler Yeats initiated
into the Isis-Urania Temple
of the Golden Dawn, 1890

8 Thursday
3rd ♏
Color: Crimson

*Lions appear often in Greek art and
mythology; the male indicates majesty while
the female grants protection*

9 Friday
3rd ♏
☽ v/c 8:51 pm
Color: Purple

10 Saturday

3rd ♏
☽ enters ♐ 5:37 am
Color: Black

Date recorded for first meeting of
Dr. John Dee and Edward Kelley, 1582

Dutch clairvoyant and psychic
healer Gerard Croiser born, 1909

○ Sunday

3rd ♐
4th quarter 11:54 pm
Color: Orange

Daylight Saving Time begins at 2 am

March

12 Monday
4th ♐
☽ v/c 2:27 pm
☽ enters ♑ 4:34 pm
Color: Silver

Stewart Edward White, psychic
researcher, born, 1873; he later
became president of the
American Society for Psychical
Research in San Francisco

13 Tuesday
4th ♑
Color: Scarlet

Magenta is a subtle color evoking intuition,
change, and spiritual healing

14 Wednesday
4th ♑
☽ v/c 4:21 pm
☽ enters ≈ 10:52 pm
Color: Brown

15 Thursday
4th ≈
Color: White

Pete Pathfinder Davis becomes the first
Wiccan priest elected as president of the
Interfaith Council of Washington State, 1995

16 Friday
4th ≈
Color: Coral

Wicked Eggs

6 hard-boiled eggs
¼ cup mayonnaise
    (or 3 tbs. ranch dressing)
Salt and pepper to taste

Shell hard-boiled eggs and cut in
half. Remove yolks, put in a bowl,
and mash thoroughly. Add mayonnaise or ranch dressing and blend
until smooth. Add salt and pepper
to taste. Scoop the yolk mixture into
the egg whites, sprinkle with paprika
if desired, and serve.

Optional:
To spice things up, add 1 teaspoon mustard, or ⅛ teaspoon cayenne, or a
few drops of hot pepper sauce. For a different sort of spiciness, add ½ teaspoon horseradish instead. Or try 1 teaspoon onion juice, or 1 tablespoon
finely minced onion.

   To make the eggs more substantial and colorful, add any or all of the
following: 2 tablespoons minced ham or deviled ham spread, 2 tablespoons
minced celery, or 2 tablespoons minced sweet pickles or pickle relish.

—Magenta Griffith

---

17 Saturday

4th ≈
☽ v/c 12:01 am
☽ enters ⓗ 1:30 am
♀ enters ♉ 6:00 pm
Color: Brown

St. Patrick's Day
Eleanor Shaw and Mary Phillips executed
in England for bewitching a woman
and her two children, 1705

☽ Sunday

4th ⓗ
☿ enters ⓗ 5:35 am
New Moon 10:42 pm
☽ v/c 11:59 pm
Color: Yellow

Solar eclipse 10:33 pm, 28° ⓗ 07'
Celtic Tree Month of Alder begins
Birthday of Edgar Cayce, psychic researcher, 1877

March

19 Monday
1st ♓
♀ enters ♈ 1:26 am
☽ enters ♈ 1:41 am
Color: Ivory

Elizabethan statute against witchcraft
enacted, 1563; this statute was replaced in
1604 by a stricter one from King James I

20 Tuesday
1st ♈
☉ enters ♈ 8:07 pm
☽ v/c 11:33 pm
Color: Red

Ostara/Spring Equinox
Sun enters Aries
International Astrology Day
Death of Lady Sheba, Wiccan author

21 Wednesday
1st ♈
☽ enters ♉ 1:15 am
Color: White

Mandate of Henry VIII against witchcraft
enacted, 1542; repealed in 1547
Green Egg magazine founded, 1968

22 Thursday
1st ♉
☽ v/c 11:12 am
Color: Green

Pope Clement urged by Phillip IV
to suppress Templar order, 1311

23 Friday
1st ♉
☽ enters ♊ 2:06 am
Color: Rose

Ostara

A time of fertility and sacred balance between night and day, Ostara begins the process when stored energy bursts forth into fruition. Feasting depends on the remaining stores of the last season's harvest, so it is not as abundant as some other sabbats. The focus of Ostara is renewal, expansion, and the return of the Sun's life-giving warmth.

Early flowers, eggs, and rabbits are all symbols of Ostara. The ancient custom of coloring and hiding eggs and rabbit symbolism both remain popular today. It is a time of celebration as the light tips the balance and overtakes night, lengthens the days, and brings anticipation of the return to the growing time.

Herbs are planted and the chores of making the soil ready for the coming planting time are begun at Ostara. Houses and lands are cleared of the winter's refuse, repairs are made, and spring cleaning is thorough and complete. This is a time of new beginnings and possibilities. New ventures are begun, new relationships are formed, and the life forces of the earth begin to awaken. Ostara is a time of deep gratitude.

—Abby Willowroot

24 Saturday

1st ♊
Color: Indigo

Birthday of Alyson Hannigan, who played Willow
on *Buffy the Vampire Slayer*
Arrest of Florence Newton, one of the few
Witches burned in Ireland, 1661

○ Sunday

1st ♊
☽ v/c 3:57 am
☽ enters ♋ 5:49 am
2nd quarter 2:16 pm
♀ enters ♓ 7:15 pm
Color: Amber

Pope Innocent III issues papal bull to
establish the Inquisition, 1199

March/April

26 Monday
2nd ♋
☽ v/c 10:36 am
Color: White

Birthday of Joseph Campbell, author
and professor of mythology, 1910

27 Tuesday
2nd ♋
☽ enters ♌ 1:04 pm
Color: Maroon

*The Buddhist gesture of blessing—hand raised
with forefinger touching the thumb—means
"perfect action of thought with perfect plan"*

28 Wednesday
2nd ♌
Color: Topaz

Scott Cunningham dies of
complications caused by AIDS, 1993

29 Thursday
2nd ♌
☽ v/c 9:24 pm
☽ enters ♍ 11:27 pm
Color: Turquoise

30 Friday
2nd ♍
Color: Pink

In Black and White

I am bruja blanca, white witch
Who knows past and future, and tells.
I am curandera, healer
Who knows herbalism and spells.
I am the one people summon
Whenever some disaster knells.

You are just a troublemaker
Full of superstition and lies.
You are in league with the Devil;
You are his lover and his prize.
The Church will root you out, bruja.
Best give up magic, if you're wise.

You say I sleep with the Devil,
But he's no friend of mine, my dear.
You curse his name but do his work;
It's me who eases pain and fear.
Tomorrow something will go wrong,
And you'll be gone, but I'll be here.

—Elizabeth Barrette

Written in the style of a Brazilian peleja poem (improvised poetic duel)

---

31 Saturday

2nd ♍︎
♇ ℞ 6:45 pm
Color: Blue

Last Witch trial in Ireland,
held at Magee Island, 1711

---

1 Sunday

2nd ♍︎
☽ v/c 9:37 am
☽ enters ♎︎ 11:43 am
Color: Yellow

Palm Sunday
April Fools' Day (All Fools' Day—Pagan)

April

☺ Monday
2nd ♎︎
Full Moon 1:15 pm
Color: White

Wind Moon

3 Tuesday
3rd ♎︎
☽ v/c 10:30 pm
Color: Red

Passover begins

4 Wednesday
3rd ♎︎
☽ enters ♏︎ 12:35 am
Color: Brown

5 Thursday
3rd ♏︎
♃ ℞ 9:22 pm
☽ v/c 10:54 pm
Color: Green

Trial of Alice Samuel, her
husband, and her daughter, who
were accused of bewitching the
wife of Sir Henry Cromwell and
several village children, 1593

6 Friday
3rd ♏︎
♂ enters ♓︎ 4:49 am
☽ enters ♐︎ 12:56 pm
Color: Rose

Good Friday
Orthodox Good Friday

Wind Moon

Ah, spring is finally here! The trees are greening, daffodils are blooming, and tulips are about to parade their candy colors. Time to bless your garden early. Take a stroll outside under the light of the rising Moon. As you walk, bless the plants by repeating the following Full Moon charm to mark your garden as an area of magic and power:

> *Under the beautiful glow of the full*
> *   Planters Moon,*
> *Elements four, gather now to hear this Witches' tune.*
> *Merge your magic with mine, circle around this space,*
> *By earth, air, fire, and water, I bless this place.*

To magically enhance any plants, seeds, and seedlings, gather and place them in the moonlight. Hold your hands over them and visualize the magic energy of creation streaming into them. Repeat this charm three times:

> *Goddess bless these seeds/plants with life, health, and vitality,*
> *I enchant these now with the power of three times three.*

—Ellen Dugan

---

7 Saturday

3rd ♐
Color: Gray

Church of All Worlds founded, 1962
First Wiccan "tract" published
by Pete Pathfinder Davis, 1996

---

8 Sunday

3rd ♐
☽ v/c 9:35 pm
☽ enters ♑ 11:36 pm
Color: Gold

Easter/Orthodox Easter
William Alexander Aynton initiated into
the Isis-Urania temple of the Golden
Dawn, 1896; he would later be called the
"Grand Old Man" of the Golden Dawn

April

9 Monday
3rd ♑
Color: Lavender

○ Tuesday
3rd ♑
4th quarter 2:04 pm
☿ enters ♈ 7:07 pm
Color: White

Passover ends
Birthday of Rev. Montague Summers,
orthodox scholar and author of
A History of Witchcraft and Demonology,

11 Wednesday
4th ♑
☽ v/c 5:57 am
☽ enters ♒ 7:23 am
♀ enters ♊ 10:15 pm
Color: Topaz

Burning of Major Weir, Scottish "sorcerer"
who confessed of his own accord, 1670;
some historians believe that the major
became delusional or senile because up
until his confession he had an excellent
reputation and was a pillar of society

12 Thursday
4th ♒
Color: Turquoise

13 Friday
4th ♒
☽ v/c 9:50 am
☽ enters ♓ 11:38 am
Color: Pink

*Orange is the color of opportunities
and adaptability; wear it when
you need a boost in imagination*

14 Saturday
4th ♓
Color: Blue

Adoption of the Principles of
Wiccan Belief at "Witch Meet"
in St. Paul, Minnesota, 1974

15 Sunday
4th ♓
☽ v/c 11:02 am
☽ enters ♈ 12:46 pm
Color: Amber

Celtic Tree Month of Willow begins

Birthday of Elizabeth Montgomery,
who played Samantha on *Bewitched*, 1933

April

16 Monday
4th ♈
Color: Ivory

Birthday of Margot Adler, author
of *Drawing Down the Moon*

☽ Tuesday
4th ♈
New Moon 7:36 am
☽ v/c 10:26 am
☽ enters ♉ 12:11 pm
Color: Scarlet

Aleister Crowley breaks into and takes over the
Golden Dawn temple, providing the catalyst for
the demise of the original Golden Dawn, 1900

18 Wednesday
1st ♉
⚥ ℞ 10:13 am
☽ v/c 10:29 pm
Color: White

19 Thursday
1st ♉
☽ enters ♊ 11:51 am
♄ D 5:24 pm
Color: Purple

Conviction of Witches
at second of four famous trials at
Chelmsford, England, 1579

20 Friday
1st ♊
☉ enters ♉ 7:07 am
Color: Coral

Sun enters Taurus

Set in Eastern Daylight Time (EDT)

Herne's Oak

An oak
Once woke
Within the hunter, Herne,
A secret need to learn
The ways his ancestors had led.
He tied great antlers to his head
And ran bare-skinned
Through wood and wind.
You can hear, even now,
His wild horn. That's how
A man unshod
Became a god.
                    —Elizabeth Barrette

Written in the style of an English hexaduad poem

---

21 Saturday

1st ♊
☽ v/c 11:52 am
☽ enters ♋ 1:50 pm
Color: Indigo

> *Geese stand for masculine power and fatherhood;*
> *serve roast goose at manhood ceremonies*

22 Sunday

1st ♋
Color: Orange

Earth Day; the first Earth Day was in 1970

April

23 Monday
1st ♋
☽ v/c 5:10 am
☽ enters ♌ 7:38 pm
Color: Silver

Edward III of England begins the
Order of the Garter, 1350

First National All-Woman Conference on
Women's Spirituality held, Boston, 1976

☾ Tuesday
1st ♌
2nd quarter 2:35 am
Color: Black

25 Wednesday
2nd ♌
Color: Yellow

USA Today reports that Patricia Hutchins
is the first military Wiccan granted
religious leave for the sabbats, 1989

26 Thursday
2nd ♌
☽ v/c 3:01 am
☽ enters ♍ 5:24 am
Color: Crimson

27 Friday
2nd ♍
☿ enters ♉ 3:16 am
Color: Purple

Avocados enhance love or lust; share one with someone special to you

Set in Eastern Daylight Time (EDT)

Superbrownies

Take your favorite brownie recipe for an 8 x 8 or 9 x 9-inch pan—even if it's a mix! Mix according to recipes or directions, but add 1 teaspoon vanilla or ½ teaspoon almond or orange extract with the liquid ingredients. Then add at least two of the following tasty extras:

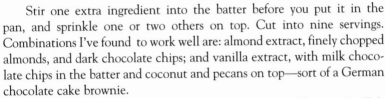

¼ cup chocolate chips
¼ cup nuts—try pecans or almonds rather than walnuts for a change
¼ cup coconut
¼ cup butterscotch or peanut butter chips
¼ cup M&Ms

Stir one extra ingredient into the batter before you put it in the pan, and sprinkle one or two others on top. Cut into nine servings. Combinations I've found to work well are: almond extract, finely chopped almonds, and dark chocolate chips; and vanilla extract, with milk chocolate chips in the batter and coconut and pecans on top—sort of a German chocolate cake brownie.

—Magenta Griffith

---

28 Saturday

2nd ♍
☽ v/c 3:14 pm
☽ enters ♎ 5:44 pm
Color: Black

A spider web evokes the power of networking and connection, and is also a potent symbol of the Goddess

---

29 Sunday

2nd ♎
Color: Yellow

Birthday of Ed Fitch, Wiccan author

April/May

30 Monday
2nd ♎
Color: White

Walpurgis Night; traditionally the
German Witches gather on the Blocksberg,
a mountain in northeastern Germany

1 Tuesday
2nd ♎
☽ v/c 4:07 am
☽ enters ♏ 6:41 am
Color: Scarlet

Beltane/May Day
Order of the Illuminati formed in
Bavaria by Adam Weishaupt, 1776

☺ Wednesday
2nd ♏
Full Moon 6:09 am
Color: Brown

Flower Moon
Birthday of D. J. Conway, Wiccan author

3 Thursday
3rd ♏
☽ v/c 2:42 am
☽ enters ♐ 6:47 pm
Color: Green

4 Friday
3rd ♐
Color: White

The *New York Herald Tribune*
carries the story of a woman who
brought her neighbor to court on
a charge of bewitchment, 1895

Beltane

Bonfires, maypoles, and Morris Dancers all celebrate the awakening of the Earth. In ancient times, there was a fear that the Earth would continue to slumber and remain fallow unless properly awoken at the Fire Festival Beltane.

Morris Dancers woke the Earth from its winter sleep by rhythmically knocking wooden staves on the ground as they danced to summon the return of bountiful crops.

Beltane is when the cares and fears of winter are sloughed off, giving way to youthful exuberance, playfulness, and sexuality. People exuberantly dance around maypoles in a symbolic representation of the union between the Goddess and the God, creating a sacred circle of abundance. Corn dollies made from the last sheaves of the previous year's crop are planted with the first seed sown.

Many bonfires are lit, often in pairs. Both humans and animals pass between two bonfires. Couples often jump over the flames to bless their union and ensure fertility, good fortune, and the blessings of the Goddess and the God.

—Abby Willowroot

---

5 Saturday

3rd ♐
Color: Gray

Cinco de Mayo
Beltane crossquarter day
(Sun reaches 15° Taurus)

---

6 Sunday

3rd ♐
☽ v/c 2:45 am
☽ enters ♑ 5:21 am
Color: Orange

Long Island Church of Aphrodite
formed by Reverend Gleb Botkin, 1938

May

7 Monday
3rd ♑
Color: Lavender

*If you dream of falling, you may be losing
your foothold on something important;
where do you feel insecure?*

8 Tuesday
3rd ♑
♀ enters ♋ 3:28 am
☽ v/c 3:34 am
☽ enters ♒ 1:48 pm
Color: Red

9 Wednesday
3rd ♒
Color: Yellow

Joan of Arc canonized, 1920

First day of the Lemuria, a Roman
festival of the dead; this festival
was probably borrowed from the
Etruscans and is one possible
ancestor of our modern Halloween

◑ Thursday
3rd ♒
4th quarter 12:27 am
☽ v/c 5:47 pm
☽ enters ♓ 7:31 pm
Color: Purple

*The mirror is an object of feminine power and
beauty, sacred to the Phoenician goddess Ishtar*

11 Friday
4th ♓
☿ enters ♊ 5:17 am
Color: Pink

Massachusetts Bay Colony Puritans
ban Christmas celebrations
because they are too Pagan, 1659

Flower Moon

This year we have two Full Moons in the month of May, which means an abundance of fairy and nature spirit activity. This month's Full Moon is also called the Dryad Moon. The Dryads are female spirits of the woodlands. These attendants of Artemis are the guardians of wild places in forests, groves, and woodlands. The Dryads are not typically seen, but their dancing energy can be sensed if you have an open mind and pure heart. To protect your yard, garden, or favorite grove of trees, call on the Dryads during the first Full Moon in May. Travel to your favorite natural place and sit quietly beneath the trees, feeling the moonlight filtering down on you. Then say the charm out loud. Remember to leave the Dryads an offering of milk and honey in thanks for their assistance.

The first Full Moon in May is a time of great power,
I call forth the Dryads to guard both leaf and flower.
Now weave your protective energy through time and space,
With laughter and joy may you guard this natural place.

—Ellen Dugan

---

12 Saturday
4th ♓
☽ v/c 7:53 pm
☽ enters ♈ 10:19 pm
Color: Brown

---

13 Sunday
4th ♈
Color: Yellow

Mother's Day
Celtic Tree Month of Hawthorn begins

May

14 Monday

4th ♈
☽ v/c 8:24 pm
☽ enters ♉ 10:48 pm
Color: Silver

*Widow Robinson of Kidderminster
and her two daughters are arrested for
trying to prevent the return of Charles II
from exile by use of magic, 1660*

15 Tuesday

4th ♉
♂ enters ♈ 10:06 am
Color: White

*White is the color of purity, innocence,
perfection, unity, and peace*

☽ Wednesday

4th ♉
New Moon 3:27 pm
☽ v/c 3:27 pm
☽ enters ♊ 10:34 pm
Color: Topaz

17 Thursday

1st ♊
Color: Turquoise

*The sphinx represents the qualities of
strength, intelligence, and mystery*

18 Friday

1st ♊
☽ v/c 8:57 pm
☽ enters ♋ 11:38 pm
Color: Coral

Set in Eastern Daylight Time (EDT)

19 Saturday
1st ♋
Color: Blue

*Cardamom seeds play a key role in Indian
and Middle Eastern cuisine; this herb
stimulates appetite and aids digestion*

20 Sunday
1st ♋
☿ ℞ 9:48 pm
Color: Gold

*Sycamore is the residence of Nut,
goddess of night and creative power;
write spells on its shed bark*

May

21 Monday

1st ♋
☽ v/c 3:46 am
☽ enters ♌ 3:56 am
☉ enters ♊ 6:12 am
Color: Ivory

Sun enters Gemini
Birthday of Gwyddion Pendderwen,
Pagan bard, 1946

22 Tuesday

1st ♌
Color: Black

Adoption of the Earth Religion
Anti-Abuse Act, 1988

☾ Wednesday

1st ♌
☽ v/c 9:08 am
☽ enters ♍ 12:26 pm
2nd quarter 5:02 pm
Color: White

Shavuot

24 Thursday

2nd ♍
♆ ℞ 9:08 pm
Color: Crimson

25 Friday

2nd ♍
☽ v/c 8:43 pm
Color: Rose

Scott Cunningham initiated into
the Traditional Gwyddonic
Order of the Wicca, 1981

Set in Eastern Daylight Time (EDT)

Cakes and Wine

Honor the gods with cakes and wine,
Mortal service to those divine.
Give to them the best, without fail.
From distant Rome did Bacchus sail,
But France is the land of the vine.
In the vineyard's rustic shrine,
Here he's worshipped, without design,
Who makes of every glass a grail.
Honor the gods.
There's flour, sifted white and fine,
And ovens glowing in a line.
The blessed cakes cooling on the rail
Mean that good fortune will prevail.
Be thankful for what's yours or mine:
Honor the gods.

—Elizabeth Barrette

Written in the style of a French lyric poem (rondeau)

---

26 Saturday

2nd ♍
☽ enters ♎ 12:16 am
Color: Indigo

---

27 Sunday

2nd ♎
Color: Amber

Birthday of Morning Glory
Zell, Church of All Worlds
Final confession of witchcraft by
Isobel Gowdie, Scotland, 1662

May/June

28 Monday

2nd ♎︎
☽ v/c 12:17 pm
☽ enters ♏︎ 1:11 pm
☿ enters ♋︎ 8:56 pm
Color: Lavender

Memorial Day (Observed)

29 Tuesday

2nd ♏︎
Color: Gray

The carp is associated with young boys in
Japanese culture, bestowing ambition and success

30 Wednesday

2nd ♏︎
☽ v/c 1:11 pm
Color: Yellow

Death of Joan of Arc, 1431

☺ Thursday
2nd ♏︎
☽ enters ♐︎ 1:06 am
Full Moon 9:04 pm
Color: White

Blue Moon

1 Friday

3rd ♐︎
Color: Coral

Witchcraft Act of 1563
takes effect in England

Set in Eastern Daylight Time (EDT)

Blue Moon

In modern folklore, a Blue Moon is the second Full Moon in one calendar month, which happens about every two years. So has the Moon actually ever appeared blue? Yes. During major volcanic eruptions, the volcanic ash rises into the atmosphere, and the ash clouds make the Moon appear blue.

For Witches today, the Blue Moon is a time of magic and mystery. On the night of a Blue Moon, the magical energy is powerful and enduring. Spells cast during a Blue Moon are said to hold until the next one. This is a fantastic time to work for love, protection, wisdom, or to try your hand at divination. A classic goddess to work with is Selene. This Greco-Roman Full Moon Goddess is generous to Witches. Light a blue candle for the Moon and a white candle for Selene. Then face the light of the Blue Moon and make your request.

> *On this night of Selene's magical Blue Moon,*
> *Lady hear my request and grant me a boon.*
> *Work your loving magic in each aspect of my life,*
> *Bless me with wisdom and protection both day and night.*

—Ellen Dugan

---

2 Saturday

3rd ♐
☽ v/c 7:29 am
☽ enters ♑ 11:09 am
Color: Blue

Birthday of Alessandro
di Cagliostro, magician, 1743

---

3 Sunday

3rd ♑
Color: Yellow

June

4 Monday

3rd ♑
❋ D 1:06 am
☽ v/c 5:43 pm
☽ enters ♒ 7:15 pm
Color: White

*Dreaming of eggs
suggests new ideas, projects, and hopes;
What are you incubating now?*

5 Tuesday

3rd ♒
♀ enters ♌ 1:59 pm
♃ enters ♉ 2:57 pm
Color: Scarlet

6 Wednesday

3rd ♒
☽ v/c 9:47 pm
Color: Brown

*Peruvian woodpeckers are believed to bring
thunderstorms with their drumming*

7 Thursday

3rd ♒
☽ enters ♓ 1:24 am
Color: Turquoise

*Blue is the color of truth and honor;
wear it to help people believe in you*

◖ Friday

3rd ♓
4th quarter 7:43 am
Color: Purple

9 Saturday

4th ♓
☽ v/c 1:52 am
☽ enters ♈ 5:26 am
Color: Gray

Birthday of Grace Cook, medium and
founder of the White Eagle Lodge, 1892

10 Sunday

4th ♈
Color: Gold

Celtic Tree Month of Oak begins

Hanging of Bridget Bishop, first to
die in the Salem Witch trials, 1692

June

11 Monday
4th ♈︎
☽ v/c 3:57 am
☽ enters ♉︎ 7:29 am
Color: Silver

12 Tuesday
4th ♉︎
☽ v/c 7:17 pm
Color: White

Masks in rituals facilitate personal
transformation, and can scare away hostile spirits

13 Wednesday
4th ♉︎
☽ enters ♊︎ 8:24 am
Color: Yellow

Birthday of William Butler Yeats, poet and
member of the Golden Dawn, 1865

Birthday of Gerald Gardner, founder
of the Gardnerian tradition, 1884

☽ Thursday
4th ♊︎
New Moon 11:13 pm
Color: Green

Flag Day

15 Friday
1st ♊︎
☽ v/c 5:59 am
☽ enters ♋︎ 9:45 am
☿ ℞ 7:40 pm
Color: Rose

Margaret Jones becomes the first person executed
as a Witch in the Massachusetts Bay Colony,
1648; she was a Boston doctor who was accused of
witchcraft after several of her patients died

Tofu Creole

1 medium onion, chopped
2 tablespoons olive oil
2 to 3 cloves garlic, minced
8 oz. tofu, cut into ½-inch cubes
2 stalks celery, chopped
6 to 8 mushrooms, sliced
½ green pepper, chopped
1 tsp. dried thyme
Dash celery salt
Black pepper and cayenne to taste
1½ to 2 cups pasta sauce, or tomato
    sauce

Sauté the onion in olive oil until just beginning to turn transparent. Add the garlic, sauté a few more minutes, then add the tofu. Once the tofu starts to sizzle, add the rest of the vegetables and sauté until softened, but not completely cooked. Add thyme and other seasonings, sauté a few more minutes, and add the pasta sauce. Cook until vegetables are tender and serve with rice.

—Magenta Griffith

---

16 Saturday

1st ♋
Color: Black

---

17 Sunday

1st ♋
☽ v/c 3:39 am
☽ enters ♌ 1:25 pm
Color: Amber

Father's Day
Birthday of Starhawk, Wiccan author

June

18 Monday
1st ♌
Color: Lavender

Church of All Worlds
chartered with the IRS, 1970

19 Tuesday
1st ♌
☽ v/c 5:22 pm
☽ enters ♍ 8:45 pm
Color: Red

*Goldenrod's botanical name, Solidago,
means "to strengthen," and in the flower
language it implies encouragement*

20 Wednesday
1st ♍
Color: Topaz

21 Thursday
1st ♍
☉ enters ♋ 2:06 pm
Color: Purple

Midsummer/Litha/Summer Solstice
Sun enters Cancer

☽ Friday
1st ♍
☽ v/c 2:50 am
☽ enters ♎ 7:43 am
2nd quarter 9:15 am
Color: White

Final witchcraft law in
England repealed, 1951

Solstice

The longest day and shortest night of the year, and known to the Druids as Alban Heruin, Solstice marks the height of the Sun's powers and the beginning of their decline as the wheel of the year turns. Celebrations are filled with marriages, music, dancing, racing, feasting, and rituals. Young animals and new babies have replenished the community. This is a joyous time of renewal.

Stonehenge was aligned to the Summer Solstice Sun about 4,000 years ago. Each year, thousands of modern Pagans and Witches gather at Stonehenge in celebration of the Summer Solstice. Many other stone-works are aligned to the Summer Solstice, attesting to the widespread importance of this day in cultures around the world.

Summer Solstice is sacred to the Horse Goddess Epona. She is a Mother Goddess of the fruits of the fields and orchards, and represents abundance; the cornucopia is a symbol of Epona's bounty

—Abby Willowroot

---

23 Saturday

2nd ♎
♅ ℞ 10:42 am
Color: Indigo

---

24 Sunday

2nd ♎
☽ v/c 3:22 pm
♂ enters ♉ 5:27 pm
☽ enters ♏ 8:26 pm
Color: Gold

Birthday of Janet Farrar, Wiccan author
James I Witchcraft Statute of 1604 is replaced in 1763 with a law against pretending to practice divination and witchcraft; law stands until 1951

25 Monday
2nd ♏
Color: Gray

A law is introduced in Germany by
Archbishop Siegfried III to encourage
conversion rather than burning of heretics, 1233

26 Tuesday
2nd ♏
☽ v/c 4:23 pm
Color: Black

Birthday of Stewart Farrar, Wiccan author

Richard of Gloucester assumes the English
throne after accusing the widowed
queen of Edward IV of witchcraft, 1483

27 Wednesday
2nd ♏
☽ enters ♐ 8:23 am
Color: White

Birthday of Scott Cunningham,
Wiccan author, 1956

28 Thursday
2nd ♐
Color: Green

29 Friday
2nd ♐
☽ v/c 1:08 pm
☽ enters ♑ 6:05 pm
Color: Pink

*Buddhists represent the body's energy
centers, or chakras, with pictures of
colored wheels or lotus blossoms*

Strong Sun Moon

June is the traditional month for weddings. One of the oldest names for this month's Full Moon is the "Mead Moon." The term "honeymoon" arose from an ancient northern European wedding custom. For the first month of marriage, newlyweds drank a daily cup of honeyed wine called mead to promote fertility. So during the Mead Moon, tap into its energies. Cast spells to promote fertility, desire, or loving relationships.

Call on Freya, the Norse goddess of love and sexuality. Her magical correspondences include amber, strawberries, and primrose. Light a golden candle for Freya, add coordinating magical items, and repeat this spell under the Full Moon to pull a little love your way:

Flowers and candles, symbols of desire and love,
Freya hear my call to you, and answer from above.
Bless my relationship, keep our love strong and true,
Guide my magic, and assist me in what I do.
For the good of all, bringing harm to none,
Under the Moon of Mead, this spell is done!

—Ellen Dugan

☺ Saturday

2nd ♑
Full Moon 9:49 am
Color: Brown

1 Sunday

3rd ♑
☽ v/c 4:45 am
Color: Yellow

July

2 Monday

3rd ♈️ ♑
☽ enters ♒ 1:24 am
Color: Lavender

3 Tuesday

3rd ♒
Color: Red

Trial of Joan Prentice, who was accused
of sending an imp in the form of a
ferret to bite children; she allegedly had
two imps named Jack and Jill, 1549

4 Wednesday

3rd ♒
☽ v/c 2:02 am
☽ enters ♓ 6:52 am
Color: Brown

Independence Day

5 Thursday

3rd ♓
♀ ℞ 6:24 am
Color: Turquoise

Conviction of Witches at third of four
famous trials at Chelmsford, England, 1589

6 Friday

3rd ♓
☽ v/c 6:08 am
☽ enters ♈ 10:56 am
Color: White

Scott Cunningham is initiated into
the Ancient Pictish Gaelic Way, 1981

Avatars of Enlightenment

She comes at first as Sita, chaste,
Her power but a faint foretaste.

As bright Parvati, she brings forth
A newborn world from south to north.

When Shakti rises like a snake,
The kundalini starts to wake

And Sarasvati brings the light
Of knowledge to dispel the night.

Then blithe Bhairavi goes astray,
And lets the demons have their way.

When Durga rides her tiger in,
The tide of battle turns again

Till Kali dances at the close
And brings to all the last repose.
—Elizabeth Barrette

Written in the style of nazm, an Indian poetic form

◑ Saturday

3rd ♈
4th quarter 12:53 pm
Color: Blue

---

8 Sunday

4th ♈
☽ v/c 9:06 am
☽ enters ♉ 1:54 pm
Color: Orange

Celtic Tree Month of Holly begins

July

9 Monday
4th ♉
☿ D 10:15 pm
Color: White

Death of Herman Slater,
proprietor of Magickal Childe
bookstore in New York, 1992

Birthday of Amber K, Wiccan author

10 Tuesday
4th ♉
☽ v/c 12:54 pm
☽ enters ♊ 4:10 pm
Color: Black

11 Wednesday
4th ♊
Color: Topaz

In German folklore, thorn trees are called
"wishing thorn" and promise divine sanctuary
and guidance

12 Thursday
4th ♊
⚷ D 3:38 am
☽ v/c 5:12 pm
☽ enters ♋ 6:39 pm
Color: Purple

Scarab beetles in Egyptian hieroglyphics
indicate deities, mythological events, historical
personages, and funeral signs

13 Friday
4th ♋
Color: Rose

Birthday of Dr. John Dee, magician, 1527

☽ **Saturday**

4th ♋

New Moon 8:04 am

☽ v/c 8:04 am

♀ enters ♍ 2:23 pm

☽ enters ♌ 10:43 pm

Color: Brown

First crop circles recorded
on Silbury Hill, 1988

15 Sunday

1st ♌

Color: Gold

July

16 Monday
1st ♌
☽ v/c 11:55 pm
Color: Gray

17 Tuesday
1st ♌
☽ enters ♍ 5:39 am
Color: Scarlet

First airing of *The Witching Hour*, a
Pagan radio show hosted by Winter
Wren and Don Lewis, on station
WONX in Evanston, Illinois, 1992

18 Wednesday
1st ♍
Color: White

19 Thursday
1st ♍
☽ v/c 9:44 am
☽ enters ♎ 3:53 pm
Color: Crimson

Rebecca Nurse hanged in
Salem, Massachusetts, 1692

20 Friday
1st ♎
Color: Pink

Pope Adrian VI issues a papal bull to the
Inquisition to re-emphasize the 1503
bull of Julius II calling for the purging
of "sorcerers by fire and sword," 1523

Invoking Danu

I invoke almighty Danu
Danu, the Goddess of Earth
Earth that rises from the water
Water that rains through the air
Air that feeds the fire
Fire that quickens my heart
Heart that drums in my body
Body that knows how to dance
Dance that raises power
Power that spins in the circle
Circle that mirrors the Moon
Moon that lights the sky
Sky that roofs the world
World that is my home
Home that smells of life
Life that gives off energy
Energy that fuels the magic
Magic that we raise, you and I
I invoke almighty Danu.
—Elizabeth Barrette

Written in Conachlann form, a medieval Irish poem

---

21 Saturday
1st ♎
Color: Indigo

Pink is the color of compassion, harmony,
affection, spiritual healing, morality, and
contentment

◖ Sunday
1st ♎
2nd quarter 2:29 am
☽ v/c 2:29 am
☽ enters ♏ 4:18 am
Color: Amber

Northamptonshire Witches
condemned, 1612

First modern recorded sighting
of the Loch Ness Monster, 1930

July

23 Monday
2nd ♏
☉ enters ♌ 1:00 am
Color: Silver

Sun enters Leo

24 Tuesday
2nd ♏
☽ v/c 6:30 am
☽ enters ♐ 4:29 pm
Color: White

25 Wednesday
2nd ♐
Color: Yellow

Death of Pope Innocent VIII, who issued
bull *Summis Desiderantes Affectibus*, 1492

26 Thursday
2nd ♐
☽ v/c 8:13 pm
Color: Green

Confession of Chelmsford Witches at first
of four famous trials at Chelmsford, 1566;
the others were held in 1579, 1589, and
1645; "Witch Finder General" Matthew
Hopkins presided at the 1645 trials

27 Friday
2nd ♐
☽ enters ♑ 2:21 am
♀ ℞ 1:28 pm
Color: Coral

Jennet Preston becomes the first of the
"Malkin Tower" Witches to be hung; she
was convicted of hiring Witches to help
her murder Thomas Lister, 1612

Set in Eastern Daylight Time (EDT)

Blessing Moon

The Full Moon in July heralds in the time of thunderstorms and the hottest days of the year, called the "dog days of summer." In ancient Egypt, the dog star, Sithor, rose with the sun the most extreme summer heat. This star was considered a second sun, which they believed added to the heat. Egyptians celebrated the "dog days" because, when the star rose with the sun, the Nile's annual flood would commence and bring life

back to the land. In this time, it's easy to have short tempers and little patience. Under this Thunder Moon, you could work for patience, peace, and, of course, a cooling summer shower.

Under this steamy Thunder Moon so bright,
I call for patience, peace, and calm this night.
May a cooling summer rain come bless the land soon,
Bringing relief, and joy to the earth, like a boon.
For the good of all, with harm to none,

By the Thunder Moon this spell is done!

—Ellen Dugan

28 Saturday
2nd ♑
☽ v/c 10:23 pm
Color: Black

☺ Sunday
2nd ♑
☽ enters ♒ 9:13 am
Full Moon 8:48 pm
Color: Yellow

Blessing Moon
Agnes Waterhouse, one of the Chelmsford
Witches, is hanged under the new witchcraft
statute of Elizabeth I, 1566; she was accused of
having a spotted cat familiar named Sathan

July/August

30 Monday
3rd ≈
Color: Ivory

Conrad of Marburg is murdered on the open
road, presumably because he had shifted from
persecuting poor heretics to nobles, 1233

31 Tuesday
3rd ≈
☽ v/c 7:55 am
☽ enters ✦ 1:40 pm
Color: Red

Birthday of H. P. Blavatsky, founder
of the Theosophical Society, 1831

Date of fabled meeting of British
Witches to raise cone of power to stop
Hitler's invasion of England, 1940

1 Wednesday
3rd ✦
Color: Brown

Lammas/Lughnasadh
Birthday of Edward Kelley,
medium of Dr. John Dee, 1555
AURORA Network UK founded, 2000

2 Thursday
3rd ✦
☽ v/c 11:36 am
☽ enters ♈ 4:43 pm
Color: Turquoise

Birthday of Henry Steele Olcott,
who cofounded the Theosophical
Society with H. P. Blavatsky, 1832

3 Friday
3rd ♈
Color: White

Lughnasadh

Lammas celebrates the first wheat or barley harvest of the year and the skills of those who tend them. Baking and sharing bread, feasting with neighbors, and honoring the still-powerful forces of the summer sun's light, and are key elements of this cooperative, community-based sabbat.

Corn and wheat dollies made from the last sheaves and stalks of harvested grain are kept through winter to be planted with the first seeds of spring. These organic Goddess figures powerfully affirm the reverence for the Earth's cycles of birth, death, and renewal. The celebrations, which feature a break from toil, contests of skill, laughter, feasting, and dancing, are tempered by the knowledge that most crops are still growing in the fields with no guarantee of adequate abundance for the long winter.

Lughnasadh's energy of cautious optimism and a feeling of well-being bring out the best in all people. The sabbat mingles the expansion of vibrant summer energy with the gathering energy of the upcoming season. The result is a unique time for solidly expanding toward focused goals, such as perfecting and challenging your skills.

—Abby Willowroot

---

4 Saturday

3rd ♈
☿ enters ♌ 1:15 pm
☽ v/c 1:31 pm
☽ enters ♉ 7:16 pm
Color: Gray

The camel has great endurance;
keep a brass camel on your altar for patience

☽ Sunday

3rd ♉
4th quarter 5:19 pm
Color: Orange

Celtic Tree Month of Hazel begins

August

6 Monday
4th ♉
☽ v/c 9:50 pm
☽ enters ♊ 10:01 pm
♃ D 10:04 pm
Color: Lavender

*In Pompeii, snakes represented household
gods—the Lares and Penates—
and the gods of fertility*

7 Tuesday
4th ♊
♂ enters ♊ 2:01 am
Color: Scarlet

8 Wednesday
4th ♊
♀ ℞ enters ♌ 9:10 pm
Color: White

Lammas crossquarter day
(Sun reaches 15° Leo)

9 Thursday
4th ♊
☽ v/c 1:27 am
☽ enters ♋ 1:36 am
Color: Green

*Yarrow grants courage and protection;
its dried flowers make attractive arrangements*

10 Friday
4th ♋
☽ v/c 8:57 am
Color: Pink

Set in Eastern Daylight Time (EDT)

Gazpacho

6 cups tomato juice
3 tbs. lemon juice
¼ cup olive oil
1 tsp. soy sauce
2 to 3 cloves garlic, finely minced or
    pressed through a garlic press
1 cucumber, finely chopped or
    shredded
1 cup carrots, shredded
1 cup celery, finely chopped
1 green pepper, finely chopped or
    shredded
¼ cup green onion or chives, chopped
2 large tomatoes, chopped

Combine liquids and mix until blended. Add vegetables. Chill overnight, or at least a few hours. You can experiment with how finely you chop vegetables. Or you can use a food processor, which is easier, but will turn the gazpacho into a puree. I prefer the interesting textures of the different ingredients. Making gazpacho is a lovely way to use up tomatoes and other garden vegetables.

—Magenta Griffith

---

11 Saturday

4th ♋
☽ enters ♌ 6:42 am
Color: Blue

Laurie Cabot withdraws from Salem,
Massachusetts, mayoral race, 1987
Birthday of Edain McCoy, Wiccan author

☽ Sunday

4th ♌
New Moon 7:02 pm
Color: Yellow

Yellow is the color of fruitfulness, beneficence, and truth

August

13 Monday
1st ♌
☽ v/c 9:34 am
☽ enters ♍ 2:03 pm
Color: Silver

Aradia de Toscano allegedly
born in Volterra, Italy, 1313

Church of Wicca founded in Australia
by Lady Tamara Von Forslun, 1989

14 Tuesday
1st ♍
Color: Gray

15 Wednesday
1st ♍
☽ v/c 5:02 pm
Color: Topaz

Birthday of Charles Godfrey Leland,
author of *Aradia, Gospel of Witches*, 1824

16 Thursday
1st ♍
☽ enters ♎ 12:04 am
Color: White

Wheat is sacred to Demeter, Greek goddess of
grain; use wheat ears in spells for abundance

17 Friday
1st ♎
Color: Rose

Scott Cunningham's first
initiation into Wicca, 1973

Set in Eastern Daylight Time (EDT)

18 Saturday

1st ♎

☽ v/c 8:21 am
☽ enters ♏ 12:13 pm
Color: Indigo

Father Urbain Grandier found
guilty of bewitching nuns at a
convent in Loudoun, France, 1634

19 Sunday

1st ♏

☿ enters ♍ 9:01 am
Color: Gold

John Willard and Reverend
George Burroughs put to death
in the Salem Witch trials, 1692

August

○ Monday

1st ♏
2nd quarter 7:54 pm
☽ v/c 9:34 pm
Color: Ivory

Execution of Lancashire Witches, 1612
Birthday of H. P. Lovecraft, horror
writer and alleged magician, 1890
Birthday of Ann Moura, author and Witch

21 Tuesday

2nd ♏
☽ enters ♐ 12:44 am
Color: Red

22 Wednesday

2nd ♐
Color: Yellow

Pope John XXII orders the
Inquisition at Carcassonne to seize
the property of Witches, sorcerers, and
those who make wax images, 1320

23 Thursday

2nd ♐
☉ enters ♍ 8:08 am
☽ v/c 8:54 am
☽ enters ♑ 11:20 am
Color: Purple

Sun enters Virgo

24 Friday

2nd ♑
☽ v/c 7:41 pm
Color: Coral

Set in Eastern Daylight Time (EDT)

A Radiant Path

The Moon has a mystery
And the Witches have a Queen.
In Italian history
They are heard, but rarely seen.
Gathered, they worship nightly
In the silver light serene.
Their magic beckons brightly,
Its power guarding the world …
Though some folk say not rightly.
Still they answer the owl's call
Aradia's chosen, all.
　　　　　—Elizabeth Barrette

Written in the style of an Italian madrigal

---

25 Saturday
2nd ♑
☽ enters ♒ 6:35 pm
Color: Black

---

26 Sunday
2nd ♒
Color: Amber

According to Japanese lore, the plum tree stands
for female purity and sacrifice rewarded

August/September

27 Monday
2nd ≈
☽ v/c 9:23 pm
☽ enters ♓ 10:34 pm
Color: Gray

Bergamot oil has a refreshing citrus scent;
aromatherapists value its cooling
and antidepressant effects

☺ Tuesday
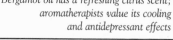

2nd ♓
Full Moon 6:35 am
Color: Scarlet

Corn Moon
Lunar eclipse 6:38 am, 4° ♓ 46'

29 Wednesday

3rd ♓
☽ v/c 6:22 pm
Color: White

Election of Pope Innocent VIII, who issued the
papal bull *Summis Desiderantes Affectibus*, 1484

30 Thursday

3rd ♓
☽ enters ♈ 12:24 am
Color: Crimson

31 Friday

3rd ♈
Color: Purple

Birthday of Raymond Buckland,
who, along with his wife, Rosemary,
is generally credited with bringing
Gardnerian Wicca to the United States

Corn Moon

We are now in the zodiac sign of Virgo, the Virgin. Virgo is known as both an Earth Goddess and a Corn Maiden, which coordinates nicely with the start of the harvest.

One of the older names for the Full Moon in August was the Wort Moon. Wort is an old Anglo-Saxon word that means "herb." During the hot and long days of summer, keep your herb gardens watered well and cared for to survive the heat. At this full "Wort Moon," you can begin to harvest your tender herbs and enchant them for various spell-work. As you go to hang them up to dry and preserve, recite this cheerful Garden Witch's charm to sustain their magic:

> *Under Virgo's full Wort Moon of yellow-gold,*
> *May the magic within these drying herbs hold.*
> *I call on the earth, fire, water, and wind,*
> *Let my Witch's herbal enchantment begin.*
> *To bring love, comfort, to protect and heal,*
> *With these rhyming words, the spell will now seal.*

—Ellen Dugan

---

1 Saturday

3rd ♈
☽ v/c 1:18 am
☽ enters ♉ 1:35 am
Color: Brown

---

2 Sunday

3rd ♉
♄ enters ♍ 9:49 am
☽ v/c 8:47 pm
Color: Yellow

Celtic Tree Month of Vine begins
Birthday of Reverend Paul
Beyerl, Wiccan author

September

◯ Monday

3rd ♉
☽ enters ♊ 3:30 am
4th quarter 10:32 pm
Color: Lavender

Labor Day

4 Tuesday

4th ♊
Color: Red

Ants are social insects, bringing the energy of
teamwork and community spirit;
keep images of them at your workplace

5 Wednesday

4th ♊
☽ v/c 7:00 am
☽ enters ♋ 7:08 am
☿ enters ♎ 8:02 am
Color: Topaz

6 Thursday

4th ♋
☽ v/c 1:04 pm
Color: Green

The aspen, a tree of protection, can teach
how to create strong psychic shields;
plant aspens to guard your home

7 Friday

4th ♋
♇ D 10:54 am
☽ enters ♌ 12:59 pm
Color: White

Roman temples and palaces use mosaic floors
to honor the movement and color of the sea,
the realm of Neptune

8 Saturday

4th ♌
♀ D 12:14 pm
♅ enters ♏ 11:30 pm
Color: Gray

Founding of the Theosophical
Society by H. P. Blavatsky, Henry
Steele Olcott, and others, 1875

9 Sunday

4th ♌
☽ v/c 2:07 pm
☽ enters ♍ 9:10 pm
Color: Orange

September

10 Monday
4th ♍
Color: White

Birthday of Carl Llewellyn
Weschcke, owner and president
of Llewellyn Worldwide

☽ Tuesday
4th ♍
New Moon 8:44 am
Color: Maroon

Solar eclipse 8:32 am, 18° ♍ 25'
Birthday of Silver RavenWolf,
Wiccan author

12 Wednesday
1st ♍
☽ v/c 12:14 am
☽ enters ♎ 7:31 am
Color: Yellow

13 Thursday
1st ♎
Color: Turquoise

Rosh Hashanah
Ramadan begins

14 Friday
1st ♎
☽ v/c 12:10 pm
☽ enters ♏ 7:37 pm
Color: Rose

Phillip IV of France draws up
the order for the arrest of
the French Templars, 1306

Birthday of Henry Cornelius Agrippa,
scholar and magician, 1486

Apple Crisp

⅓ cup flour
1 cup rolled oats
½ cup brown sugar
2 tsp. cinnamon
¼ tsp. nutmeg
¼ tsp. ginger
¼ cup butter (half a stick)
4 cups sliced apples

Preheat oven to 375 degrees F. Mix dry ingredients in a bowl, then cut butter into mixture to make topping. Place apples—peeled, cored and thinly sliced—into a 9-inch pie plate or 8-inch square pan. Spread topping evenly over the apples and gently press to form a crust. Bake about half an hour, or until slightly browned. Serve warm or cold, with ice cream if desired.

—Magenta Griffith

15 Saturday

1st ♏
Color: Blue

16 Sunday

1st ♏
☽ v/c 7:40 pm
Color: Gold

*Black is the color of binding, death,
female power, and protection*

September

17 Monday
1st ♏
☽ enters ♐ 8:21 am
Color: Silver

Bewitched debuts on ABC-TV, 1964

18 Tuesday
1st ♐
Color: White

If you dream about cooking something,
consider the ways you use your energy to
make things palatable

☽ Wednesday
1st ♐
☽ v/c 12:48 pm
2nd quarter 12:48 pm
☽ enters ♑ 7:51 pm
Color: Topaz

20 Thursday
2nd ♑
♀ ℞ 9:05 am
Color: Purple

21 Friday
2nd ♑
Color: Pink

Friends may exchange cat's-eye rings as a
pledge of platonic affection

Mabon

A sabbat of balance and equality, Mabon is a time of second harvest and work shared. Day and night are the same length. A dynamic tension exists that seems to stretch time into both a long day and a long night.

The second harvest is complete and the winter's supply is becoming known. Joyous celebrations flow in abundant years and a more subdued gratitude in years of lesser harvests. There is a collective sigh as the road ahead becomes clearer and planning for the coming winter begins.

Celebrated around the world, this sabbat borders summer and winter—the last day of the growing sun, the moment before the light will be overtaken by night. The energy of Mabon is similar to the electrically charged energy that occurs just before twilight, the energy of Between-Time.

Mabon is a time of strong and clear psychic visions and dreams. Spirit is clear and contemplation comes easily. It is a time of powerful, mature insight and dynamic action rooted in past efforts. Combining psychic visions with grounded effort leads to some interesting paths and journeys. Autumnal equinox, like vernal equinox, is a time of unlimited possibilities.

—Abby Willowroot

22 Saturday

2nd ♑
☽ v/c 2:15 am
☽ enters ♒ 4:18 am
Color: Indigo

Yom Kippur

23 Sunday

2nd ♒
☉ enters ♎ 5:51 am
Color: Amber

Mabon/Fall Equinox
Sun enters Libra

September

24 Monday
2nd ♒
☽ v/c 5:14 am
☽ enters ♓ 8:55 am
Color: Ivory

25 Tuesday
2nd ♓
Color: Gray

U.S. Senate passes an amendment (705)
attached by Senator Jesse Helms to House
Resolution 3036 (1986 budget bill),
denying tax-exempt status to any organization
that espouses satanism or witchcraft, 1985

☻ Wednesday
2nd ♓
☽ v/c 8:31 am
☽ enters ♈ 10:22 am
Full Moon 3:45 pm
Color: Yellow

Harvest Moon
Joan Wiliford hanged at Faversham,
England, 1645; she testified that
the Devil came to her in the form of a
black dog that she called "Bunnie"

27 Thursday
3rd ♈
☿ enters ♏ 1:17 pm
Color: White

Sukkot begins

28 Friday
3rd ♈
☽ v/c 9:58 am
☽ enters ♉ 10:17 am
♂ enters ♋ 7:54 pm
Color: Coral

Harvest Moon

Traditionally the Harvest Moon occurs at the Full Moon closest to the Autumnal Equinox. The Harvest Moon usually looks larger than other Full Moons because cooler fall air curves the light near the horizon. The fabulous reddish-orange color associated with the Harvest Moon is the result of seeing the dust, dirt, and pollen in the lower atmosphere as you gaze across the horizon.

The night of the Harvest Moon is a perfect time to celebrate the season of the harvest and to take a moment to reflect on what you are thankful for, such as freedom, friends, home, and family. Set up a pretty altar full of seasonal accessories such as apples, grapes, acorns, miniature pumpkins, and colorful fall leaves. Light an orange candle for the harvest season and repeat this Harvest Moon blessing.

Beneath the light of the Harvest Moon so bright,
I am thankful for many blessings tonight.
I celebrate the bounty of the good green earth,
Lord and Lady bless me, granting health, peace, and mirth.

—Ellen Dugan

---

29 Saturday

3rd ♉
Color: Black

---

30 Sunday

3rd ♉
☽ v/c 1:10 am
☽ enters ♊ 10:34 am
Color: Yellow

Celtic Tree Month of Ivy begins

October

1 Monday
3rd ♊
Color: Gray

Birthday of Isaac Bonewits,
Druid, magician, and Witch

Birthday of Annie Besant,
Theosophical Society president, 1847

2 Tuesday
3rd ♊
☽ v/c 6:51 am
☽ enters ♋ 12:57 pm
Color: Red

Birthday of Timothy Roderick,
Wiccan author

◑ Wednesday
3rd ♋
4th quarter 6:06 am
☽ v/c 4:41 pm
Color: Brown

Sukkot ends

4 Thursday
4th ♋
☽ enters ♌ 6:27 pm
Color: Turquoise

President Ronald Reagan signs JR 165
making 1983 "The Year of the Bible"
(public law #9728Q); the law states that the
Bible is the word of God and urges a return
to "traditional" Christian values, 1982

5 Friday
4th ♌
Color: White

Equatorial Enhancements

Look around. The jungle has eyes:
Mambang Angin, spirit of wind,
Teasing the fools, leading the wise
On quests of knowledge with no end.

Mambang Angin, spirit of wind,
Beckons from walls of waving green.
On quests of knowledge with no end
We come and go, unheard, unseen.

Beckoning from walls that wave green,
Teasing the fools, leading the wise,
We come and go, unheard, unseen.
Look around. The jungle has eyes.
—Elizabeth Barrette

Written in the style of a Malaysian pantun poem

---

6 Saturday

4th ♌
Color: Black

---

7 Sunday

4th ♌
☽ v/c 1:28 am
☽ enters ♍ 3:03 am
Color: Orange

Birthday of Arnold Crowther, stage
magician and Gardnerian Witch, 1909

October

8 Monday

4th ♍
♀ enters ♍ 2:53 am
Color: Lavender

Columbus Day (observed)

9 Tuesday

4th ♍
☽ v/c 7:08 am
☽ enters ♎ 1:57 pm
Color: White

*The griffin means invincibility,
which is why they're popular
as guardians bracketing driveways and doors*

10 Wednesday

4th ♎
Color: Topaz

☽ Thursday

4th ♎
New Moon 1:01 am
☽ v/c 7:22 pm
Color: Green

*If you dream of a besom, you may need to
create a sacred space for yourself,
or sweep your space clean*

12 Friday

1st ♎
☿ ℞ 12:00 am
☽ enters ♏ 2:13 am
Color: Rose

Birthday of Aleister Crowley, 1875

Set in Eastern Daylight Time (EDT)

13 Saturday

1st ♏
☽ v/c 5:23 pm
Color: Gray

Ramadan ends

Jacques de Molay and other
French Templars arrested by
order of King Phillip IV, 1306

14 Sunday

1st ♏
☽ enters ♐ 2:58 pm
Color: Yellow

October

15 Monday
1st ♐
Color: White

16 Tuesday
1st ♐
☽ v/c 8:32 pm
Color: Black

The apple relates to Freya (Asatru), Aphrodite (Greek), and Eris (Roman); its qualities include beauty, liberty, mystery, and discord

17 Wednesday
1st ♐
☽ enters ♑ 3:03 am
Color: Brown

Brown is the color of stability, justice, animals, grounding, neutrality, and decision-making

18 Thursday
1st ♑
Color: Crimson

Birthday of Nicholas Culpepper, astrologer and herbalist, 1616

◑ Friday
1st ♑
⚴ enters ♑ 3:38 am
2nd quarter 4:33 am
☽ v/c 4:33 am
☽ enters ♒ 12:52 pm
Color: Pink

Set in Eastern Daylight Time (EDT)

Bread Pudding

Some people use pudding at Samhain for divination—they add little tokens, like a thimble for productivity, a coin for money, a little horseshoe for luck. Whoever gets the coin will have money in the coming year, etc.

2 cups bread crumbs (use a food processor to make from leftover bread)
3 eggs
2¼ cups milk
½ tsp. almond extract
⅓ cup sugar
¼ cup chocolate chips

Butter a 1½-quart baking dish. Place bread crumbs in buttered dish. Mix eggs, milk, almond extract, and sugar. Pour the mixture over crumbs, then sprinkle with chocolate chips. If you wish, add tokens at this time. Let stand about a half hour. Put 1 inch of water in a large shallow pan, place the baking dish in this, and bake at 350 degrees F for about an hour. Serve warm.

—Magenta Griffith

---

20 Saturday

2nd ≈
Color: Blue

Birthday of Selena Fox, Circle Sanctuary

21 Sunday

2nd ≈
☽ v/c 3:36 pm
☽ enters ♓ 7:02 pm
Color: Amber

Spearmint strengthens mental powers and grants protection during sleep

---

22 Monday

2nd ♓
Color: Silver

*Burn beeswax candles in spells for success
or career to take advantage of the
industrious energy of bees*

23 Tuesday

2nd ♓
☉ enters ♏ 3:15 pm
☽ v/c 4:17 pm
☽ enters ♈ 9:24 pm
☿ enters ♎ 11:36 pm
Color: Maroon

Sun enters Scorpio

24 Wednesday

2nd ♈
Color: Yellow

25 Thursday

2nd ♈
☽ v/c 5:46 pm
☽ enters ♉ 9:07 pm
Color: Purple

Jacques de Molay first interrogated
after Templar arrest, 1306

☺ Friday

2nd ♉
Full Moon 12:51 am
Color: Coral

Blood Moon
De Molay and thirty-one other Templars
confess to heresy in front of an assembly of
clergy; all later recant their confessions, 1306
Sybil Leek dies of cancer, 1982

Blood Moon

The Full Moon in October is often called the Hunter's Moon. During ancient times, hunters were respected as the tribe's life-givers for they supplied the food. In Britain, Herne the Hunter is a deity of the "Dark Forest." Lord of the woodland and its animals, Herne oversees all of nature and the results of fertility for both the natural world and men. Herne, described as a large, virile man crowned with the antlers of a stag and purportedly wears furs and carries a wooden bow, is often accompanied by a pack of hunting dogs.

As our nights grow noticeably longer and autumn commences, consider working with Herne for courage and the ability to "hunt down" your path in life. His wisdom is vast, and, if you listen, he can help you find your way while traveling along your own magical path, even in the darkest of times.

As the Hunter's Moon lights up the October sky,
Herne protect me, the dark time of the year is nigh,
Help me to find my own path, and to gain knowledge true,
May I walk with wisdom and strength in all that I do.

—Ellen Dugan

---

27 Saturday

3rd ♉
☽ v/c 3:15 am
☽ enters ♊ 8:11 pm
Color: Indigo

Circle Sanctuary founded, 1974

---

28 Sunday

3rd ♊
Color: Gold

Celtic Tree Month of Reed begins

October/November

29 Monday

3rd ♊
☽ v/c 3:50 pm
☽ enters ♋ 8:49 pm
Color: Ivory

MacGregor Mathers issues manifesto calling himself supreme leader of the Golden Dawn; all members had to sign an oath of fealty to him, 1896

Birthday of Frater Zarathustra, who founded the Temple of Truth in 1972

30 Tuesday

3rd ♋
Color: Red

House-Senate conferees drop the Senate provision barring the IRS from granting tax-exempt status to groups that promote satanism or witchcraft, 1985

PACT (Pagan Awareness Coalition for Teens) established in Omaha, Nebraska, 2001

31 Wednesday

3rd ♋
☿ D 9:57 am
☽ v/c 1:13 pm
♆ D 4:07 pm
Color: White

Samhain/Halloween

Martin Luther nails his ninety-five theses to the door of Wittenburg Castle Church, igniting the Protestant revolution, 1517

Covenant of the Goddess founded, 1975

○ Thursday

3rd ♋
☽ enters ♌ 12:48 am
4th quarter 5:18 pm
☿ D 6:58 pm
Color: Green

All Saints' Day

Aquarian Tabernacle Church established in the United States, 1979

2 Friday

4th ♌
Color: Pink

Circle Sanctuary purchases land for nature preserve, 1983

Samhain

At the beginning of the Witches' New Year, the nights grow long, the winds chill, and the cold winter begins. To celebrate this final harvest, meat is put up; root crops, nuts, and apples are stored; and the year's activities draw to a close. Debts are paid, old things are cleaned, mended, or discarded. The house is swept clean and old brooms are thrown out and replaced by new brooms to make sure no bad luck follows the household into the new year.

The air crackles with energy and excitement as the veil between the worlds is thin, spirits are near, and power is in the air. This is a night to celebrate the Witch and practice a few ancestral customs. Covens and solitaries celebrate this sabbat with reverence, joy, and magical workings.

Spirits are easily contacted, and debts to those who have passed over are paid in the form of food offerings left at crossroads. The different realms are more easily accessed now, including the faery realm. Care must be taken not to offend or disrespect the dead, the Fey, or other beings beyond our own plane of existence.

—Abby Willowroot

---

3 Saturday
4th ♌
☽ v/c 3:13 am
☽ enters ♍ 8:44 am
Color: Brown

---

4 Sunday
4th ♍
Color: Yellow

Daylight Saving Time ends at 2 am

November

5 Monday
4th ♍
☽ v/c 1:10 pm
☽ enters ♎ 6:47 pm
Color: Gray

6 Tuesday
4th ♎
Color: Black

Election Day (general)

7 Wednesday
4th ♎
Color: Topaz

Samhain crossquarter day
(Sun reaches 15° Scorpio)

8 Thursday
4th ♎
☽ v/c 1:46 am
☽ enters ♏ 7:18 am
♀ enters ♎ 4:05 pm
Color: White

Sentencing of Witches in
Basque Zugarramurdi trial, 1610

Marriage of Patricia and Arnold Crowther
officiated by Gerald Gardner, 1960

☽ Friday
4th ♏
New Moon 6:03 pm
☽ v/c 10:19 pm
Color: Purple

Patricia and Arnold Crowther
married in civil ceremony, 1960

10 Saturday

1st ♏
☽ enters ♐ 7:59 pm
Color: Blue

In China, deer represent honor and success

11 Sunday

1st ♐
☿ enters ♏ 3:41 am
Color: Orange

Veterans Day

November

12 Monday
1st ♐
Color: Lavender

A cluster of smoky quartz absorbs negativity

13 Tuesday
1st ♐
☽ v/c 2:53 am
☽ enters ♑ 8:00 am
Color: Maroon

A zigzag line can represent the course of life,
or the element of water

14 Wednesday
1st ♑
Color: Yellow

15 Thursday
1st ♑
♂ ℞ 3:24 am
☽ v/c 4:19 am
☽ enters ♒ 6:30 pm
Color: Turquoise

Aquarian Tabernacle Church
established in Canada, 1993

16 Friday
1st ♒
Color: Coral

Night of Hecate

Set in Eastern Standard Time (EST)

Dangergelders

Heroes in hard times
Hail their trials!
Some seek Valhalla's
Shining vale and
Pride of place among
Past mighty ones.
Others only want
Oaths in this world
Fulfilled fully, deeds
Found in duty.
Cheer the challenge met,
Chased by magic,
Roped by runes seething,
Racked by strong hands.
Gods give us worries –
Gladly we rise!

     —Elizabeth Barrette

Written in the style of fornyr'islag (a Norse, free verse form)

◯ Saturday
1st ≈
2nd quarter 5:32 pm
☽ v/c 9:51 pm
Color: Indigo

Birthday of Israel Regardie, occultist
and member of the OTO, 1907

---

18 Sunday
2nd ≈
☽ enters ♓ 2:14 am
Color: Gold

Aleister Crowley initiated into the
Golden Dawn as Frater Perdurabo, 1898

November

19 Monday
2nd ♓
Color: Ivory

Birthday of Theodore
Parker Mills, Wiccan elder, 1924

20 Tuesday
2nd ♓
☽ v/c 2:26 am
☽ enters ♈ 6:24 am
Color: Red

Church of All Worlds
incorporates in Australia, 1992

21 Wednesday
2nd ♈
Color: Brown

22 Thursday
2nd ♈
☽ v/c 3:40 am
☽ enters ♉ 7:18 am
☉ enters ♐ 11:50 am
Color: Purple

Thanksgiving Day
Sun enters Sagittarius

23 Friday
2nd ♉
☽ v/c 1:53 pm
Color: Rose

Birthday of Lady Tamara Von Forslun,
founder of the Church of Wicca and the
Aquarian Tabernacle Church in Australia

Mourning Moon

November is a transitional time as autumn fades and it becomes more winterlike every day. The skies may be brilliantly blue, but most leaves have fallen from the trees. In the morning, you may find that Jack Frost has been hard at work decorating windows, adorning autumn leaves, and coating blades of grass with his silvery-white frosting. Jack Frost, an elfish character connected to Norse folklore, was believed to have brought

the brilliant fall colors by nipping leaves with his frost. In Russia, he is known as the benevolent Papa Frost—a Santa type cloaked in shimmering white and silvery blue—who was thought to bind water and the earth together during the year's coldest days. Welcome the spirit of Papa Frost or Old Jack Frost into your magic and put the freeze on a troubling situation. Tonight, as the Full Moon rises, write your problem on a slip of paper, tuck it in a paper cup, fill the cup with water, and place in the freezer. Then repeat this spell:

> *Old Jack Frost put the freeze on this problem for me,*
> *Bring harm to none, and as I will, so mote it be.*

—Ellen Dugan

☺ Saturday

2nd ♉
♀ D 5:15 am
☽ enters ♊ 6:29 am
Full Moon 9:30 am
Color: Blue

Mourning Moon

---

25 Sunday

3rd ♊
Color: Orange

Celtic Tree Month of Elder begins
Dr. John Dee notes Edward
Kelley's death in his diary, 1595

November/December

26 Monday

3rd ♊
☽ v/c 2:37 am
☽ enters ♋ 6:07 am
Color: Silver

*The Phrygian two-headed eagle stands for double vision:
seeing the past and future, or both sides of an issue*

27 Tuesday

3rd ♋
☽ v/c 11:22 pm
Color: Gray

*The color gray represents neutrality,
knowledge, vision, and balance*

28 Wednesday

3rd ♋
☽ enters ♌ 8:23 am
Color: Topaz

*In Arabic and Spanish lore, the quince fruit
brings virility and masculine power*

29 Thursday

3rd ♌
Color: Crimson

30 Friday

3rd ♌
☽ v/c 12:25 pm
☽ enters ♍ 2:44 pm
Color: White

Birthday of Oberon Zell,
Church of All Worlds

Father Urbain Grandier imprisoned in
France for bewitching nuns, 1633

Aladdin's Heir

Day strikes with heavy hand
On the sun's anvil, sand,
Until gentle night comes
To soothe the scorched, dry land.

Here peacocks peck at crumbs
And in the courtyard, drums
Call out the ancient dance;
Cymbals chime on thumbs.

Tales of genie and lamp,
Ghost caravan's last camp,
Carpets flying through air,
Thieves left drowned, but not damp –

Desert magic has flair.
Who will seek it, will dare
To read the old, cracked scrolls
And be Aladdin's heir?

Dawn breaks, and daylight rolls
Over the dusty knolls.
There, enchanted, you stand
Joining historic souls.
                    —Elizabeth Barrette

Written in the style of a Persian rubaiyat poem

◗ Saturday
3rd ♍
☿ enters ♐ 7:21 am
4th quarter 7:44 am
Color: Brown

Birthday of Anodea Judith,
president, Church of All Worlds

2 Sunday
4th ♍
☽ v/c 9:12 pm
Color: Yellow

December

3 Monday
4th ♍
☽ enters ♎ 1:01 am
Color: Gray

*Athena's symbol is the olive branch,
which signifies victory or peace*

4 Tuesday
4th ♎
Color: Red

5 Wednesday
4th ♎
♀ enters ♏ 8:29 am
☽ v/c 9:48 am
☽ enters ♏ 1:31 pm
Color: Topaz

Hanukkah begins
Pope Innocent VIII reverses the
Canon Episcopi by issuing the bull
Summis Desiderantes Affectibus, removing
obstacles to Inquisitors, 1484
Death of Aleister Crowley, 1947

6 Thursday
4th ♏
Color: Turquoise

Death of Jacob Sprenger, coauthor
of the *Malleus Maleficarum*, 1495
Birthday of Dion Fortune, member
of the Golden Dawn, 1890

7 Friday
4th ♏
☽ v/c 5:16 am
Color: White

8 Saturday

4th ♏

☽ enters ♐ 2:11 am

⚹ enters ♐ 3:06 pm

Color: Blue

☽ Sunday

4th ♐

New Moon 12:40 pm

Color: Orange

In Russian folklore, the bear is the friend of
humankind, capable of giving sound advice

December

10 Monday

1st ✗
☽ v/c 10:36 am
☽ enters ♑ 1:50 pm
Color: Lavender

In Pictish temples and tomb sculptures, arches
stood for the sun and its path across the sky

11 Tuesday

1st ♑
☽ v/c 6:57 pm
Color: White

12 Wednesday

1st ♑
Color: Yellow

Hanukkah ends

13 Thursday

1st ♑
☽ enters ♒ 12:01 am
Color: Purple

First papal bull against black magic
issued by Alexander IV, 1258

14 Friday

1st ♒
Color: Pink

Dark Fruit Cake

Prepare a 9-inch loaf pan, greased and lined with waxed paper. Preheat oven to 325 degrees F. Mix the following together in a large bowl until all are well distributed.

2 cups flour
½ cup brown sugar
¼ tsp. salt
¼ tsp. nutmeg, heaped a bit
1 level tsp. cinnamon
1¼ cups dried fruit mix
½ cup raisins
¼ cup walnuts

In a separate container beat together ½ cup vegetable oil, ½ cup whole milk, and 2 eggs.

Add wet ingredients to dry, blend until flour disappears, and then stir a few more times. Put in the pan, sprinkle 2 teaspoons brown sugar on top. Bake 1½ hours. Cool completely before removing from pan. Since this recipe does not have rum, brandy, or other alcohol, it will not keep as well as traditional fruitcake. You can experiment with various fruits and nuts.

—Magenta Griffith

15 Saturday

1st ≈
☽ v/c 6:50 am
☽ enters ♓ 8:15 am
Color: Indigo

16 Sunday

1st ♓
Color: Yellow

In magic, knots represent fidelity, wisdom, and true love

December

◐ Monday
1st ♓
2nd quarter 5:17 am
☽ v/c 1:27 pm
☽ enters ♈ 1:52 pm
Color: Ivory

18 Tuesday
2nd ♈
♃ enters ♑ 3:11 pm
Color: Black

Pine trees enhance conjugal affection and longevity;
plant them in pairs or groves for best effect

19 Wednesday
2nd ♈
♄ Rx 9:09 am
☽ v/c 2:33 pm
☽ enters ♉ 4:38 pm
Color: Brown

Ruby grants power and courage, and dispels nightmares

20 Thursday
2nd ♉
☿ enters ♑ 9:43 am
♇ enters ♒ 2:12 pm
Color: Crimson

21 Friday
2nd ♉
☽ v/c 1:06 am
☽ enters ♊ 5:14 pm
Color: Purple

Use rosemary to break hexes

Long Nights Moon

This year the Winter Solstice plays a part in our December Full Moon celebration. According to midwinter mythology, this is the time of the Oak King, who lends us his name for the year's final Full Moon. At the Winter Solstice, the Oak King has defeated his brother, the Holly King, and the waxing half of the year has begun. From this point, the light will only grow stronger, and our daylight hours will grow longer.

In herbalism, the oak is a tree of wisdom, power, and magic. So on this night of the Full Oak Moon, ask the Oak King for his blessings. Find a small oak twig or acorn and set it in a place of prominence. Then arrange next to it a gold candle for illumination and a green candle to encourage prosperity. Light the candles and say:

A Full Moon night in December brings magic so true,
May the Oak King grant me wisdom in all that I do.
See the burning candles of green and gold so bright,
Light and riches they will bring on this blessed night.

—Ellen Dugan

---

22 Saturday

2nd ♊
☉ enters ♑ 1:08 am
Color: Blue

Yule/Winter Solstice
Sun enters Capricorn
Janet and Stewart Farrar begin
their first coven together, 1970

☺ Sunday

2nd ♊
☽ v/c 3:25 pm
☽ enters ♋ 5:18 pm
Full Moon 8:15 pm
Color: Amber

Long Nights Moon

December

24 Monday
3rd ♋
Color: Silver

Christmas Eve
Celtic Tree Month of Birch begins

25 Tuesday
3rd ♋
☽ v/c 8:17 am
☽ enters ♌ 6:52 pm
Color: White

Christmas Day
Feast of Frau Holle, Germanic
weather goddess who was believed
to travel through the world to
watch people's deeds; she blessed
the good and punished the bad

26 Wednesday
3rd ♌
Color: Topaz

Kwanzaa begins
Dr. Fian arraigned for twenty counts
of witchcraft and treason, 1590

27 Thursday
3rd ♌
☽ v/c 9:54 pm
☽ enters ♍ 11:44 pm
Color: Green

Birthday of Gerina Dunwich,
Wiccan author

28 Friday
3rd ♍
♃ D 6:24 pm
Color: Rose

Set in Eastern Standard Time (EST)

Yule

The longest night of the year marks the return of the Sun and the lengthening days, a time of introspection, and celebration of endurance and the powers of hope.

Winter Solstice is a time of gathering with friends, family, and neighbors to share the stored abundance of the previous harvest and make ready for the long winter ahead. This sabbat is an affirmation of hope.

Yule is both a Scandinavian and Germanic festival marking the winter holiday. The decorating of trees, the singing of songs and telling of stories, hot spiced drinks, and sacred pine boughs all have their roots in Pagan Winter Solstice and Yule practices. Deer and their association with the Horned God Cernunnos have also survived in modern celebrations. Ancient Druids harvested mistletoe from Sacred Oaks to hang in the doorway of homes to ensure the blessings of the Sacred Groves and for good luck.

The Yule log is lit, mistletoe is harvested and hung, bonfires blaze, feasting, and sharing handmade objects all take place on Winter Solstice to celebrate the passage of the longest night and the return of the Sun's power.

—Abby Willowroot

29 Saturday
3rd ♍
Color: Gray

30 Sunday
3rd ♍
☽ v/c 8:08 am
☽ enters ♎ 8:37 am
♀ enters ♐ 1:02 pm
Color: Gold

Ginger is an herb of new beginnings; eat candied ginger to gain initiative and self-confidence

December/January

◑ Monday

3rd ♎

4th quarter 2:51 am

♂ enters ♊ 11:00 am

Color: White

New Year's Eve

Castle of Countess Bathory of Hungary raided, 1610; accused of practicing black magic, she murdered scores of the local townsfolk; she was walled up in a room in her castle, where she later died

---

1 Tuesday

4th ♎

☽ v/c 7:33 pm

☽ enters ♏ 8:32 pm

Color: Maroon

New Year's Day

Kwanzaa ends

---

2 Wednesday

4th ♏

Color: White

---

3 Thursday

4th ♏

☽ v/c 7:30 pm

Color: Purple

Eight is a sacred number in India, China, and Japan because of the Eightfold Path of Buddha

---

4 Friday

4th ♏

☽ enters ♐ 9:13 am

Color: Coral

Set in Eastern Standard Time (EST)

Lifeblood

Nabia, the water goddess,
Spills her blessings all over Spain,
White foam lace along blue bodice,
Her body swollen with the rain.
All that grows here, she must sustain
Through cloud and fountain and river.
Here live the people of the plain
Who, hearing her name, still shiver.
　　　　　　　　—Elizabeth Barrette

Written in the style of a Spanish huitain poem

---

5 Saturday
4th ♐
Color: Indigo

---

6 Sunday
4th ♐
☽ v/c 7:27 pm
☽ enters ♑ 8:43 pm
Color: Orange

About the Authors

ELIZABETH BARRETTE serves as the managing editor of *PanGaia*. She has been involved with the Pagan community for more than seventeen years, and has done much networking with area Pagans including coffee-house meetings and open sabbats. Her other writing fields include speculative fiction and gender studies. In 2005, her poem "The Poltergeist of Polaris" earned a nomination for the Rhysling Award. She lives in central Illinois and enjoys herbal landscaping and gardening for wildlife.

DALLAS JENNIFER COBB lives in an enchanted waterfront village. She's freed up resources for what she loves: family, gardens, and fabulous food. When not scheming novel ways to pay the bills, she's running country roads or wandering a beach. Her essays are in recent Seal Press anthologies *Three Ring Circus* and *Far From Home*. Her video documentary *Disparate Places* appeared on TV Ontario's *Planet Parent*. Contact this regular contributor to Llewellyn's almanacs at Jennifer.Cobb@Sympatico.ca.

ELLEN DUGAN, the "Garden Witch," is a psychic-clairvoyant and a practicing Witch of twenty years. Ellen is a Master Gardener and teaches classes on flower folklore and gardening at a community college. She is the author of several Llewellyn books: *Garden Witchery, Elements of Witchcraft, 7 Days of Magic, Cottage Witchery, Autumn Equinox, The Enchanted Cat, Herb Magic for Beginners,* and *Natural Witchery*. Ellen wholeheartedly encourages folks to personalize their spell craft and to go outside and get their hands dirty, so they can discover the wonder and magic of the natural world. Ellen and her family live in Missouri.

EMELY FLAK is a practicing solitary witch from Daylesford, Australia. When she is not writing, she is at her "day job" as a learning and development professional. Recently, this busy mother of two and partner of one completed training to be a civil celebrant. Much of her work is dedicated to embracing the ancient wisdom of Wicca for personal empowerment, particularly in the competitive work environment.

MAGENTA GRIFFITH has been a Witch for nearly thirty years and is a founding member of the coven Prodea, which has celebrated rituals since 1980. She has been a member of the Covenant of the Goddess, the Covenant of Unitarian Universalist Pagans, and Church of All Worlds. She presents workshops and classes at festivals around the Midwest. She spends her spare time reading, cooking, and petting her cat.

JENNIFER HEWITSON has been a freelance illustrator since 1985. Her illustrations have appeared in local and national publications including the *Wall Street Journal*, the *Washington Post*, the *Los Angeles Times*, *US News & World Report*, and *Ladybug* magazine. She also works for advertising and packaging clients such as Disney and the San Diego Zoo. Jennifer has created a line of greeting cards for Sun Rise Publications, and has illustrated several children's books. Her work has been recognized by numerous organizations, including *Communication Arts* magazine, *Print* magazine, Society of Illustrators Los Angeles, and *How* magazine.

JAMES KAMBOS is a writer and painter interested in folk magic. He has written many articles about traditional magic used in Greece, the Middle East, and the United States. Tending his herb and flower gardens helps him celebrate the changing seasons.

LYNN SMYTHE is a freelance writer and gardener living in south Florida with her husband, son, and daughter. She is the founder and manager of the online community *Herb Witch* (groups.msn.com/herbwitch). She offers a variety of magical writing tools and supplies for sale on her website, the *Magical Scriptorium*, www.magicalscriptorium.com.

K. D. SPITZER is an experienced astrologer, teacher, and writer living on the seacoast of New Hampshire where she is always assigned the Hecate role in ritual. Known for her legendary honey cakes, Ms. Spitzer also publishes and edits *The Country Wisdom Almanac*, an uncomplicated compendium designed to bring the power of the planets to daily life.

ABBY WILLOWROOT is the founder and director of the Goddess 2000 Project, the Spiral Goddess Grove, and Willowroot Real Magic Wands. Since 1965 Abby has been a full-time professional Goddess artist, wand maker, and writer. Nine pieces of Ms. Willowroot's jewelry are in the Smithsonian Institution's permanent collection. Her work has appeared in many metaphysical publications.

Appendix

Daily Magical Influences

Each day is ruled by a planet with specific magical influences.

Monday (Moon): peace, healing, caring, psychic awareness

Tuesday (Mars): passion, courage, aggression, protection

Wednesday (Mercury): study, travel, divination, wisdom

Thursday (Jupiter): expansion, money, prosperity, generosity

Friday (Venus): love, friendship, reconciliation, beauty

Saturday (Saturn): longevity, endings, homes

Sunday (Sun): healing, spirituality, success, strength, protection

Color Correspondences

Colors are associated with each day, according to planetary influence.

Monday: gray, lavender, white, silver, ivory

Tuesday: red, white, black, gray, maroon, scarlet

Wednesday: yellow, brown, white, topaz

Thursday: green, turquoise, white, purple, crimson

Friday: white, pink, rose, purple, coral

Saturday: brown, gray, blue, indigo, black

Sunday: yellow, orange, gold, amber

Lunar Phases

Waxing, from New Moon to Full Moon, is the ideal time to do magic to draw things to you.

Waning, from Full Moon to New Moon, is a time for study, meditation, and magical work designed to banish harmful energies.

The Moon's Sign

The Moon continuously moves through each sign of the zodiac, from Aries to Pisces, staying about two and a half days in each sign. The Moon influences the sign it inhabits, creating different energies that affect our day-to-day lives.

Aries: Good for starting things. Things occur rapidly, but quickly pass. People tend to be argumentative and assertive.

Taurus: Things begun now last longest, tend to increase in value, and become hard to change. Brings out an appreciation for beauty and sensory experience.

Gemini: Things begun now are easily changed by outside influence. Time for shortcuts, communication, games, and fun.

Cancer: Stimulates emotional rapport between people. Supports growth and nurturing. Tend to domestic concerns.

Leo: Draws emphasis to the self, to central ideas or institutions, away from connections with others and emotional needs.

Virgo: Favors accomplishment of details and commands from higher up. Focus on health, hygiene, and daily schedules.

Libra: Favors cooperation, compromise, social activities, balance, friendship, and partnership.

Scorpio: Increases awareness of psychic power. Precipitates psychic crises and ends connections thoroughly. People tend to brood and become secretive.

Sagittarius: Encourages confidence and flights of imagination. This is an adventurous, philosophical, and athletic Moon sign. Favors expansion and growth.

Capricorn: Develops strong structure. Focus on traditions, responsibilities, and obligations. A good time to set boundaries and rules.

Aquarius: Rebellious energy. Time to break habits and make abrupt change. Personal freedom and individuality is the focus.

Pisces: The focus is on dreaming, nostalgia, intuition, and psychic impressions. A good time for spiritual or philanthropic activities.

2007 Eclipses

March 3, 6:22 pm; Lunar eclipse 13° ♍ 00'
March 18, 10:33 pm; Solar eclipse 28° ♓ 07'
August 28, 6:38 am; Lunar eclipse 4° ♓ 46'
September 11, 8:32 am; Solar eclipse 18° ♍ 25'

2007 Full Moons

Cold Moon: January 3, 8:57 am
Quickening Moon: February 2, 12:45 am
Storm Moon: March 3, 6:17 pm
Wind Moon: April 2, 1:15 pm
Flower Moon: May 2, 6:09 am
Blue Moon: May 31, 9:04 pm
Strong Sun Moon: June 30, 9:49 am
Blessing Moon: July 29, 8:48 pm
Corn Moon: August 28, 6:35 am
Harvest Moon: September 26, 3:45 pm
Blood Moon: October 26, 12:51 am
Mourning Moon: November 24, 9:30 am
Long Nights Moon: December 23, 8:15 pm

Planetary Retrogrades in 2007

Planet		Begin		—	Direct		
Saturn	℞	12/05/06	11:06 pm	—	Direct	04/19/07	5:24 pm
Mercury	℞	02/13/07	11:38 pm	—	Direct	03/07/07	11:44 pm
Pluto	℞	03/31/07	6:45 pm	—	Direct	09/07/07	10:54 am
Jupiter	℞	04/05/07	9:22 pm	—	Direct	08/06/07	10:04 pm
Neptune	℞	05/24/07	9:08 pm	—	Direct	10/31/07	4:07 pm
Mercury	℞	06/15/07	7:40 pm	—	Direct	07/09/07	10:15 pm
Uranus	℞	06/23/07	10:42 am	—	Direct	11/24/07	5:15 am
Venus	℞	07/27/07	1:28 pm	—	Direct	09/08/07	12:14 pm
Mercury	℞	10/12/07	12:00 am	—	Direct	11/01/07	6:58 pm
Mars	℞	11/15/07	3:24 am	—	Direct	01/30/08	5:33 pm
Saturn	℞	12/19/07	9:09 am	—	Direct	05/02/08	11:07 pm

Set in Eastern Time. All times corrected for Daylight Saving Time.

Moon Void-of-Course Data for 2007

Last Aspect		New Sign	
Date	Time	Sign	New Time

JANUARY

Date	Time	Sign	New Time
2	5:06 am	2 ♋	10:14 am
3	8:57 am	4 ♌	4:14 pm
6	7:55 pm	7 ♍	1:18 am
9	7:51 am	9 ♎	1:15 pm
11	8:56 pm	12 ♏	2:08 am
14	10:49 am	14 ♐	1:11 pm
16	4:28 pm	16 ♑	8:49 pm
18	11:01 pm	19 ♒	1:15 am
21	12:00 am	21 ♓	3:48 am
23	2:11 am	23 ♈	5:52 am
25	4:50 am	25 ♉	8:28 am
27	11:08 am	27 ♊	12:10 pm
29	1:40 pm	29 ♋	5:16 pm
30	4:30 pm	2/1 ♌	12:14 am

FEBRUARY

Date	Time	Sign	New Time
1/30	4:30 pm	1 ♌	12:14 am
3	5:55 am	3 ♍	9:34 am
5	5:37 am	5 ♎	9:15 pm
8	6:38 am	8 ♏	10:09 am
10	5:39 am	10 ♐	10:01 pm
13	3:45 am	13 ♑	6:42 am
14	10:24 pm	15 ♒	11:34 am
17	11:14 am	17 ♓	1:30 pm
19	11:43 am	19 ♈	2:06 pm
21	12:42 pm	21 ♉	3:03 pm
23	2:46 pm	23 ♊	5:42 pm
25	8:21 pm	25 ♋	10:47 pm
27	1:03 am	28 ♌	6:29 am

MARCH

Date	Time	Sign	New Time
2	2:02 pm	1 ♍	4:32 pm
5	1:56 am	5 ♎	4:25 am
7	2:51 pm	7 ♏	5:16 pm
9	8:51 pm	10 ♐	5:37 am
12	2:27 pm	12 ♑	4:34 pm
14	4:21 pm	14 ♒	10:52 pm
17	12:01 am	17 ♓	1:30 am
18	11:59 pm	19 ♈	1:41 am
20	11:33 pm	21 ♉	1:15 am
22	11:12 am	23 ♊	2:06 am
25	3:57 am	25 ♋	5:49 am
26	10:36 am	27 ♌	1:04 pm
29	9:24 pm	29 ♍	11:27 pm

APRIL

Date	Time	Sign	New Time
1	9:37 am	1 ♎	11:43 am
3	10:30 pm	4 ♏	12:35 am
5	10:54 pm	6 ♐	12:56 pm
8	9:35 am	8 ♑	11:36 pm
11	5:57 am	11 ♒	7:23 am
13	9:50 am	13 ♓	11:38 am
15	11:02 am	15 ♈	12:46 pm
17	10:26 am	17 ♉	12:11 pm
18	10:29 pm	19 ♊	11:51 am
21	11:52 am	21 ♋	1:50 pm
23	5:10 am	23 ♌	7:38 pm
26	3:01 am	26 ♍	5:24 am
28	3:14 pm	29 ♎	5:44 pm

MAY

Date	Time	Sign	New Time
1	4:07 am	1 ♏	6:41 am
3	2:42 am	3 ♐	6:47 pm
6	2:45 am	6 ♑	5:21 am
8	3:34 am	8 ♒	1:48 pm
10	5:47 pm	10 ♓	7:31 pm
12	7:53 pm	12 ♈	10:19 pm
14	8:24 pm	14 ♉	10:48 pm
16	3:27 pm	16 ♊	10:34 pm
18	8:57 pm	18 ♋	11:38 pm
21	3:46 am	21 ♌	3:56 am
23	9:08 am	23 ♍	12:26 pm
25	8:43 pm	26 ♎	12:16 am
28	12:17 pm	28 ♏	1:11 pm
30	1:11 pm	31 ♐	1:06 am

JUNE

Date	Time	Sign	New Time
2	7:29 am	2 ♑	11:09 am
4	5:43 pm	4 ♒	7:15 pm
6	9:47 pm	7 ♓	1:24 am
9	1:52 am	9 ♈	5:26 am
11	3:57 am	11 ♉	7:29 am
12	7:17 pm	13 ♊	8:24 am
15	5:59 am	15 ♋	9:45 am
17	3:39 am	17 ♌	1:25 pm
19	5:22 pm	19 ♍	8:45 pm
22	2:50 am	22 ♎	7:43 am
24	3:22 pm	24 ♏	8:26 pm
26	4:23 pm	27 ♐	8:23 am
29	1:08 pm	29 ♑	6:05 pm

JULY

Date	Time	Sign	New Time
1	4:45 am	2 ♒	1:24 am
4	2:02 am	4 ♓	6:52 am
6	6:08 am	6 ♈	10:56 am
8	9:06 am	8 ♉	1:54 pm
10	12:54 pm	10 ♊	4:10 pm
12	5:12 pm	12 ♋	6:39 pm
14	8:04 pm	14 ♌	10:43 pm
16	11:55 pm	17 ♍	5:39 am
19	9:44 am	19 ♎	3:53 pm
22	2:29 am	22 ♏	4:18 am
24	6:30 am	24 ♐	4:29 pm
26	8:13 pm	27 ♑	2:21 am
28	10:23 pm	29 ♒	9:13 am
31	7:55 am	31 ♓	1:40 pm

AUGUST

Date	Time	Sign	New Time
2	11:36 am	2 ♈	4:43 pm
4	1:31 pm	4 ♉	7:16 pm
6	9:50 pm	6 ♊	10:01 pm
9	1:27 am	9 ♋	1:36 am
10	8:57 am	11 ♌	6:42 am
13	9:34 am	13 ♍	2:03 pm
15	5:02 am	16 ♎	12:04 am
18	8:21 am	18 ♏	12:13 pm
20	9:34 pm	21 ♐	12:44 am
23	8:54 am	23 ♑	11:20 am
24	7:41 pm	25 ♒	6:35 pm
27	9:23 pm	27 ♓	10:34 pm
29	6:22 pm	30 ♈	12:24 am

SEPTEMBER

Date	Time	Sign	New Time
1	1:18 am	1 ♉	1:35 am
2	8:47 pm	3 ♊	3:30 am
5	7:00 am	5 ♋	7:08 am
6	1:04 pm	7 ♌	12:59 pm
9	2:07 pm	9 ♍	9:10 pm
12	12:14 am	12 ♎	7:31 am
14	12:10 pm	14 ♏	7:37 pm
16	7:40 pm	17 ♐	8:21 am
19	12:48 pm	19 ♑	7:51 pm
22	2:15 am	22 ♒	4:18 am
24	5:14 am	24 ♓	8:55 am
26	8:31 pm	26 ♈	10:22 am
28	9:58 am	28 ♉	10:17 am
30	1:10 am	30 ♊	10:34 am

OCTOBER

Date	Time	Sign	New Time
2	6:51 am	2 ♋	12:57 pm
3	4:41 pm	4 ♌	6:27 pm
7	1:28 am	7 ♍	3:03 am
9	7:08 am	9 ♎	1:57 pm
11	7:22 pm	12 ♏	2:13 am
13	5:23 pm	14 ♐	2:58 pm
16	8:32 pm	17 ♑	3:03 am
19	4:33 am	19 ♒	12:52 pm
21	3:36 pm	21 ♓	7:02 pm
23	4:17 pm	23 ♈	9:24 pm
25	5:46 pm	25 ♉	9:07 pm
27	3:15 pm	27 ♊	8:11 pm
29	3:50 pm	29 ♋	8:49 pm
31	1:13 pm	11/1 ♌	12:48 am

NOVEMBER

Date	Time	Sign	New Time
10/31	1:13 pm	1 ♌	12:48 am
3	3:13 am	3 ♍	8:44 am
5	1:10 pm	5 ♎	6:47 pm
8	1:46 am	8 ♏	7:18 am
9	10:19 pm	10 ♐	7:59 pm
13	2:53 am	13 ♑	8:00 am
15	4:19 am	15 ♒	6:30 pm
17	9:51 pm	18 ♓	2:14 am
20	2:26 am	20 ♈	6:24 am
22	3:40 am	22 ♉	7:18 am
23	1:53 pm	24 ♊	6:29 am
26	2:37 am	26 ♋	6:07 am
27	11:22 pm	28 ♌	8:23 am
30	12:25 pm	30 ♍	2:44 pm

DECEMBER

Date	Time	Sign	New Time
2	9:12 pm	3 ♎	1:01 am
5	9:48 am	5 ♏	1:31 pm
7	5:16 am	8 ♐	2:11 am
10	10:36 am	10 ♑	1:50 pm
11	6:57 pm	13 ♒	12:01 am
15	6:50 am	15 ♓	8:15 am
17	1:27 pm	17 ♈	1:52 pm
19	2:33 pm	19 ♉	4:38 pm
21	1:06 am	21 ♊	5:14 pm
23	3:25 pm	23 ♋	5:18 pm
25	8:17 pm	25 ♌	6:52 pm
27	9:54 pm	27 ♍	11:44 pm
30	8:08 am	30 ♎	8:37 am

Name:

Address, City, State, Zip:

Home Phone: Office Phone:

E-mail: Birthday:

Name:

Address, City, State, Zip:

Home Phone: Office Phone:

E-mail: Birthday:

Name:

Address, City, State, Zip:

Home Phone: Office Phone:

E-mail: Birthday:

Name:

Address, City, State, Zip:

Home Phone: Office Phone:

E-mail: Birthday:

Name:

Address, City, State, Zip:

Home Phone: Office Phone:

E-mail: Birthday:

Name:

Address, City, State, Zip:

Home Phone: Office Phone:

E-mail: Birthday:

Name:

Address, City, State, Zip:

Home Phone: Office Phone:

E-mail: Birthday:

Name:

Address, City, State, Zip:

Home Phone: Office Phone:

E-mail: Birthday:

Name:

Address, City, State, Zip:

Home Phone: Office Phone:

E-mail: Birthday:

Name:

Address, City, State, Zip:

Home Phone: Office Phone:

E-mail: Birthday:

Name:

Address, City, State, Zip:

Home Phone: Office Phone:

E-mail: Birthday:

Name:

Address, City, State, Zip:

Home Phone: Office Phone:

E-mail: Birthday:

Name:

Address, City, State, Zip:

Home Phone: Office Phone:

E-mail: Birthday:

Name:

Address, City, State, Zip:

Home Phone: Office Phone:

E-mail: Birthday:

Name:

Address, City, State, Zip:

Home Phone: Office Phone:

E-mail: Birthday:

Name:

Address, City, State, Zip:

Home Phone: Office Phone:

E-mail: Birthday:

Name:

Address, City, State, Zip:

Home Phone: Office Phone:

E-mail: Birthday:

Name:

Address, City, State, Zip:

Home Phone: Office Phone:

E-mail: Birthday:

Name:

Address, City, State, Zip:

Home Phone: Office Phone:

E-mail: Birthday:

Name:

Address, City, State, Zip:

Home Phone: Office Phone:

E-mail: Birthday:

Name:

Address, City, State, Zip:

Home Phone: Office Phone:

E-mail: Birthday:

Name:

Address, City, State, Zip:

Home Phone: Office Phone:

E-mail: Birthday:

Name:

Address, City, State, Zip:

Home Phone: Office Phone:

E-mail: Birthday:

Name:

Address, City, State, Zip:

Home Phone: Office Phone:

E-mail: Birthday:

Name:

Address, City, State, Zip:

Home Phone: Office Phone:

E-mail: Birthday:

Name:

Address, City, State, Zip:

Home Phone: Office Phone:

E-mail: Birthday:

Name:

Address, City, State, Zip:

Home Phone: Office Phone:

E-mail: Birthday:

Name:

Address, City, State, Zip:

Home Phone: Office Phone:

E-mail: Birthday:

Name:

Address, City, State, Zip:

Home Phone: Office Phone:

E-mail: Birthday:

Name:

Address, City, State, Zip:

Home Phone: Office Phone:

E-mail: Birthday:

Name:

Address, City, State, Zip:

Home Phone: Office Phone:

E-mail: Birthday: